# A
# LIVING HOPE

# A
# LIVING HOPE

*The Comfort and Assurance That Comes*
*from Knowing God Cares for You*

DAVID HANEY

CROSSWAY BOOKS • WHEATON, ILLINOIS
A DIVISION OF GOOD NEWS PUBLISHERS

*A Living Hope*

Copyright © 1999 by David Haney

Published by Crossway Books
        a division of Good News Publishers
        1300 Crescent Street
        Wheaton, Illinois 60187

Cover photo: Masterfile Corporation / Gloria H. Chomica

Cover design: Cindy Kiple

First printing 1999

Printed in the United States of America

Scripture taken from the *Holy Bible: New International Version*®. Copyright © 1973, 1978, 1984 by International Bible Society. Used by permission of Zondervan Publishing House. All rights reserved.

The "NIV" and "New International Version" trademarks are registered in the United States Patent and Trademark Office by International Bible Society. Use of either trademark requires the permission of International Bible Society.

**Library of Congress Cataloging-in-Publication Data**
Haney, David, 1956-
    A living hope / David Haney.
       p.   cm.
    Includes bibliographical references.
    ISBN 1-58134-040-0 (tpb. : alk. paper)
    1. Hope—Religious aspects—Christianity.   I. Title.
    BV4638.H28   1999
    234'.25—dc21                   98-44038
                                      CIP

| 15 | 14 | 13 | 12 | 11 | 10 | 09 | 08 | 07 | 06 | 05 | 04 | 03 | 02 | 01 | 00 | 99 |
| 15 | 14 | 13 | 12 | 11 | 10 | 9 | 8 | 7 | 6 | 5 | 4 | 3 | 2 | 1 |

*To Robin Hardy*
*a writer's writer*
*Without her persistence and*
*professionalism, this book would*
*never have come to be.*

# CONTENTS

# ACKNOWLEDGMENTS

*To my Trinity Bible Church family:*

You are an example of grace and a people of hope. It is my greatest honor to serve you as your pastor and shepherd.

To Mark Jones, Rick Pierce, James Wartian, Kim Talkington, David Wolf, Diane Ruse, Debbie Foster, Charleen Huber, Vicki Frank, and Jane Honett—the staff team at TBC. You make each day of ministry a joy. Your loyalty and support allow me to be better in ministry than I have any right to be.

To the elders, deacons, and hundreds of other leaders, teachers, and servants whose ministry of love and sacrificial service brings great glory and honor to the great God we serve—thank you.

*To my new friends at Crossway Books:*

Lane Dennis, Marvin Padgett, Lila Bishop, and the staff at Crossway—thank you for taking a chance and renewing my hope.

*To my girls:*

Cayah, Leah, and Kaitlyn Haney—you own my heart, and for you I have such great hope.

To my life partner, Diane—for me there is no other. I am thankful beyond words for your loyal love and for your unfailing hope.

# INTRODUCTION

It was a portrait of hopelessness—people aimlessly wandering or standing awkwardly, hollow stares varnished over their faces. Each room of the large suburban home cloistered small congregations of grief. It was a day of vivid impressions and unclear details recorded vaguely on the tearstained canvas of my memory.

It was a day I can barely remember; yet it was a day I cannot seem to forget. I remember the suffocating weight of grief. I remember the sights and the sounds of people's desperate search for hope. While I cannot remember every detail of those hours, I will never forget the lesson about hope that I learned that day.

## THE WEIGHT OF GRIEF

His sandy brown hair rarely seemed combed, but it suited him. He may have grown up on city streets, but he belonged on country roads. He lived with asphalt under his feet, but there were hayseeds in his blood and straw in his boots. He was a pickup-drivin', fish-catchin', fun-lovin' young good old boy. He went off and married his college sweetheart, and just as soon as they could, they moved out of that there big city. He and his young bride started a beautiful family, and he began his career with dirt under his fingernails and the hot sun on the back of his neck, and it suited him.

It may be impossible to say exactly why he sat down in his living room one evening, placed a .44 magnum to his head, and ended his life while his wife and young children prepared dinner around the corner. Professional therapists, psychiatrists, and psychologists would certainly have their educated opinions. Anthropologists, sociologists, and theologians could offer other reasons. Counselors, friends, and family members would have still more. Yet no one can know for certain. It is even possible that were you able to ask him, he could not tell you exactly what caused him to make such a tragic decision.

Strangely enough, through the haze of unclear memories of that day, I remember quite distinctly one thing someone said to me. We were staring outside through the kitchen window as if the hope we were searching for could be found just beyond the glass, like oxygen just beyond the reach of a drowning man. While the activity of grief carried on behind us, this one, whose identity I cannot remember, said about this one I cannot forget, "I guess he just lost his hope."

I am certain that I acknowledged the wisdom of the statement, and as I continued to visit with others, I filed his observation away with all the other meaningless observations about incomprehensible events like this. But over the years this observation has seemed to transcend that moment.

### STORMS ON THE HORIZON OF HOPE

Most of us know the feeling that comes with losing hope. Many of us have felt it in our hearts. We have seen it sweep in on our lives and in on the lives of others. We have sensed its approach as we might sense a change in the weather. We have watched the clouds of frustration gather and felt the winds of discouragement rise. Every direction we might look, the horizon of our future grows darker. At times like these, we don't need a meteorologist to tell us that a storm is moving in. It is a storm of hopelessness.

Many people know from their personal experience how painful it is to have no hope—to have no hope left in their careers or their marriages or finances or health or the future. The weight of hopelessness is similar to the weight of grief. A loss of hope can feel like a loss of life.

We all realize, whether we have given it much thought or not, that a loss of hope is a bad thing. Most of us would agree that a loss of hope can be a discouraging, depressing, and even downright painful thing. But until I had reflected upon that hazy afternoon of grief, I had never considered that a loss of hope could be a fatal thing.

## Living in a Land of
## Lost Hope

If it is dangerous or even fatal for an individual to lose hope, what happens when an entire generation is without hope? What happens when an entire society, a culture, or a nation slips into hopelessness? Consider for a moment the possibility that those of us living in the predominately hassle-free, relatively safe luxury of twentieth-century America are, when it comes to the reality of hope, as bad off as the most impoverished and brutalized people on earth.

Obviously, most Americans do not live with the fear that our homes will be overrun by hostile forces or that we will have to carry our children to refugee camps on our backs. Most Americans do not face the possibility that roving hordes of rebel militia will wipe out our communities while we sleep. While hunger, disease, and crime touch our lives, we are certainly not suffering like those in a nation at war or in an impoverished third world country. Or are we?

We may not be starving, but we are going hungry. Our cities are not being leveled by bombs, but each day families are blowing apart. We may not be at war, but we live in a culture fighting for its life. We live in a nation where hope is dying and the number of casualties and prisoners of war rises every day.

### THE GENERATION OF ALIENATION

As we consider the data collected from the 38-million-member generation born approximately between 1965 and 1983, we can see the evidence of a growing storm. A generation is in danger of losing its hope.

In the "The Whatever Generation," "The Baby Busters," "The Generation Xers" the seeds of the previous generation's discontent and rebellion have sprouted. The seeds of skepticism, cynicism, hedonism, and rebellion planted by the "Baby Boomers" have grown up to produce a bitter fruit in their own children, and it is the fruit of hopelessness.

The evidence seems to indicate that the Xers' parents have by and large walked away from the foundations that gave hope to their own

parents and grandparents. Commitment to traditionally hope-enrich-
ing institutions such as the family, the community, and the church
have been devalued and abandoned by this post-World War Two generation. Is it any surprise then that their children find themselves feeling alienated and lost, wandering in a wilderness of hopelessness?

## THE STATISTICS OF ALIENATION

This alienation and apathy is suggested by two frightening sets of
statistics. The first is the number of young people ending their own
lives. Suicide is the third leading killer of fifteen- to twenty-four-year-
olds in America. While the rates seem to have leveled out in the past
five years, they are up an astonishing 200 percent over the last four
decades.[1] In 1960 the teen suicide rate was 3.6 deaths per 100,000.
In the 1980s when the first of this generation entered the fifteen- to
nineteen-year-old age group, the teen suicide rate more than doubled
to 8.5 deaths per 100,000. And by 1990 this tragic rate had almost
tripled to 11.3 deaths per 100,000.[2]

For every adolescent suicide, it is estimated that there are between
fifty and one hundred suicides attempted. Add to this the fact that
drug overdoses and alcohol-related automobile fatalities are usually
termed "accidental," and it becomes apparent that there is a significant
struggle in the hearts of American adolescents. If there is one act that
represents a complete loss of hope, it is the act of deliberate self-
destruction.

### The Poet Turns Prophet

On Tuesday, April 5, 1994, Gen-X rock poet Kurt Cobain ended his
own life. Two days after his body was discovered, more than 5,000
people gathered outside of his Seattle home for a candlelight vigil. The
next week 20,000 copies of the album *Nevermind* were sold. His iden-
tification with his generation had tragically come full circle.

In an article for *The Dallas Observer* written shortly after Cobain's
death, reporter Robert Wilonsky made some poignant observations:

> One colleague suggests Cobain's suicide will be our genera-
> tion's equivalent to the assassination of Kennedy: we're all

going to realize everything means nothing. . . . Cobain only drove home a point we knew all along: everything's disposable in our culture, even our greatest musicians.

Cobain's death leaves this tremendous gaping hole. Whether you liked Nirvana or not, whether you believe they were our generation's Beatles, his suicide only reinforces the belief that nothing is good enough anymore. Kurt joined a band . . . made a million bucks in one year, got married and had himself a kid, saw the world, and it still wasn't enough.

"I haven't felt the excitement for so many years," Cobain wrote in his suicide note. "The worst crime I can think of is to fake it."[3]

While Kurt Cobain may or may not be a hero of his generation, he was one of its most popular poets, spokespersons, and leaders. And while he may not even be all that typical of those his age, his life flashes as a warning light on the dashboard of our culture telling us that something here is not okay. And to those of us who are concerned about the future of our children and our society, it may be time to find out what is really wrong.

## Hopelessness and Lawlessness

If the first indication that we are living in a land that has lost its hope is a growing sense of disillusionment that at its extreme expresses itself in suicide, then the second indication is increasing disobedience and disrespect—that at its extreme expresses itself in senseless violence and crime.

When there is no hope, there is no reason for discipline or obedience. If tomorrow doesn't matter, if the future holds nothing but more pain, then what motivation is there to do what is right? Hopelessness leads to lawlessness. When hope goes, anything goes. When you believe that it can't get any worse, there is no reason not to do the worst. Without a future, the matters of the moment are all that matters, and therefore there is no reason not to do whatever seems right at the moment.

Imagine a prison inmate sentenced to death with no possibility of appeal. His death is certain; there is no hope of pardon. Suppose then that he escapes and makes his way to your house. What is there to stop him from doing whatever he wants? Already under a death sentence, he has no fear because he has no future. How could you stop him? What could you pay him or threaten him with to make him surrender? He is already a dead man. He has no hope, and in his hands, neither do you.

There are an increasing number of young people in our society who feel as if they are already sentenced to death. They have lost all hope, and in some sense they are already dead. Once again brutal statistics illustrate the depth of this loss of hope.

### The Rise of the Super Predators

All across the nation, in every segment of our society, crime has increased significantly over the past forty years. While the population of America has increased by 41 percent since 1960, the number of violent crimes—murders, rapes, robberies, and aggravated assaults—has increased 550 percent.[4] Statistically, eight out of ten Americans can expect to be victims of violent crimes at least once in their lives.[5] And the fastest-growing segment of the criminal population is our nation's children.[6]

According to the National Crime Survey, almost three million crimes occur on or near school campuses every year—16,000 per school day, or one every six seconds.[7]

Between 1982 and 1991 the arrest rate of juveniles for murder increased 93 percent, compared with a 16-percent increase among adults.[8]

From 1960 to 1991 the rate of homicide deaths among children under age nineteen has more than quadrupled.[9]

In just the five years between 1987 and 1991, according to the Department of Justice, the number of teenagers arrested for murder rose 85 percent.

According to the FBI, in 1991 more than 2,200 murder victims were under the age of eighteen—an average of more than six young people killed every day.

The Justice Department estimated in 1993 that nearly one million people between the ages of twelve and nineteen were raped, robbed, or assaulted, often by their peers.[10]

Statistics predict that the generation entering adolescence near the turn of the century could push the percentage of juvenile murderers to 25 by the year 2005.[11]

Homicide is now far and away the leading cause of death among African-American teenagers.[12] A young black man living in Harlem is less likely to live until the age of forty than a man in Bangladesh.[13]

Yet, shocking as these statistics are, the most frightening problem is the rising percentage of teens who kill or maim without "moral compunction." These teens, often referred to as "super predators" have been raised on the streets. They have no conscience and know nothing but a culture of violence. These teenage and preteen criminals take another person's life as easily as they might take a wallet.

Judge David Grossman of Cincinnati, the president of a national juvenile judges' group, describes this growing number of juveniles as "undisciplined, untutored, unnurtured young people."

Kathleen Heide, a Florida psychotherapist and criminologist, describes these young people as "incapable of empathy."

John Firman of the International Association of Chiefs of Police perfectly identifies these young criminals as "kids with no hope, no fear, no rules and no life expectancy."[14]

We may be living in a land that lies directly in the path of a violent storm of hopelessness. The generation of young Americans moving into adolescence and adulthood is struggling with difficult issues on a scale unfamiliar to previous generations. And if this generation is struggling more than any before it to find a genuine hope, what of *their* children?

## LOOKING FOR A FALSE HOPE

No one can survive for long without any hope at all. Even the most jaded individual hides in his heart a hope of some kind—the hope for recognition, popularity, or fame. The hope of wealth or success. The hope of a better life or of a different life. The hope of faith. The hope of love. God has designed us so that we cannot exist without hope.

This desperate search for hope can be found not only in America's youth but also in every generation, in every philosophical and political persuasion, and in every subculture in our society.

## HOW TO START YOUR OWN CULT

This may help us begin to understand how a man who seems to be somewhat eccentric, if not completely insane, can become a guru or a cult leader. We may ask ourselves, "Why do people follow such a wacko?" or "How can these seemingly intelligent people be so blind to this egotistical idiot's agenda?"

These are not necessarily stupid people; these are desperate people. In the psychological and sometimes theological diatribes of these self-proclaimed messiah wannabes is a promise of something no one can live without, and it's not money; it's not sex; it's not happiness. These things are not compelling enough to cause people to leave everything and follow a stranger to their deaths if need be. No, the message is more powerful. At its root the message offers hope. It doesn't need to be a true hope. With desperate people, any half-baked substitute will do.

## RIPE FOR DECEPTION

We are a society desperate for hope and therefore ripe for deception. Our headlong pursuit of hope often defies logic. Sexual promiscuity in the face of disease, unsatisfying materialism at the expense of relationships, and an unending fascination with the escapist fantasy of entertainment are all symptomatic of a society in denial.

In a 1994 survey, George Barna found that 72 percent of all Americans believe that "there is no such thing as absolute truth." This number stood at 80 percent among those people age twenty-five years and younger.[15] Yet at the same time, 92 percent of all Americans either believe it to be "very desirable or somewhat desirable to have a close relationship with God."[16]

The contradiction here becomes apparent when we realize that without absolute truth, there is no absolute hope. Without a fixed reference point, our hope becomes as situational and transitory as our circumstances. If nothing is absolutely certain, we cannot be absolutely certain of anything. And while a clear majority of people realize that a relationship with God is desirable, by denying the possibility of unchanging truth, they deny His ability to provide an unchanging hope.

## LOSING OUR LAST HOPE

In 1994–95 a book by Robert Preston titled *The Hot Zone* topped the best-seller lists for over thirty weeks. It was a riveting true story of a virus—not just any virus, but the Ebola virus. This virus had surfaced in the small village of Kikwit, Zaire, in central Africa. Preston's book, along with the fictional movie *Outbreak*, horrified millions with the graphic portraits of this fatal and untreatable virus on the loose.

Little is known at this time about the origins of the Ebola virus or how it is transmitted in humans. We only know that up to 90 percent of those who are infected die within a matter of days. As with other viral diseases ranging from the common influenza virus to the rare and obscure Oropouche virus, the only protection is prevention, and the only prevention is by vaccination.

However, vaccinations do not exist for every virus. For example, there is no vaccination for the HIV virus. Where a vaccination does exist, the threat of an uncontrolled outbreak is minimal, but only if the vaccination is available and is used. In our technologically sophisticated world, it is absurd, paranoid, and conspiratorial to think that an existing vaccine would be withheld from people fighting a deadly virus.

Imagine for a moment, in light of all we have considered in this introduction, that hopelessness is a fatal virus transmitted through a godless culture. It can be easily passed from generation to generation, house to house, and person to person. A hopeful person infected by this virus can quickly become completely hopeless.

If hopelessness were indeed a microbiological disease, we would have to say that we are facing an outbreak of epidemic proportions. This potentially fatal disease attacks the spirit and soul of its victims, blinding them, paralyzing them, isolating them, and eventually killing them.

But you don't have to imagine that we have a vaccine for this disease of hopelessness. We do. As with any vaccination, it works by injecting a small amount of the inactivated virus into the body. A vaccine against hopelessness is made up of a "defeated" form of the same virus. Once the body learns how to fight off the virus through the preparation of the vaccine, it becomes immune to widespread infection. Thus, in this analogy, we could say that the vaccination for hopelessness is fashioned from the defeat of hopelessness, from the cells of hope discovered by those who have triumphed over seemingly hopeless circumstances.

Now imagine that we possessed an unlimited supply of this vaccine and not only stood by and watched as our culture became terminally infected, but then we too found ourselves suffering from the same disease. Unfortunately, we do not need too much imagination. We only need clear vision.

The epidemic is not only around us; it is also among us.

## THE HOPELESS CHRISTIAN

Why then do so many believers struggle to maintain hope?

Why do the moral convictions of Christians differ so little from those of unbelievers?

Why are the followers of Jesus Christ as likely to be at a loss for hope as those in the world they are to reach?

### The Infection of Hopelessness

According George Barna's 1994 survey, 72 percent of all adults in America agree that "there is no such thing as absolute truth."[17] This creeping moral relativism should not surprise us. We have lived for the past few decades under the philosophical guidance of situational ethics. The "if it feels good, do it," "no harm, no foul," "it doesn't hurt anyone" system of values is totally flexible and circumstantial. Absolute truth has to take a hike in a land of equal opportunity values.

What should disturb us, however, are the figures among those who identified themselves as "born-again" Christians. Among this group 62 percent agree that "there is no such thing as absolute truth." And even among those who identified themselves narrowly as "evangelicals," 44 percent agree with the statement.[18] If the disease of hopelessness is infecting the body of Christ, this is the point of infection.

To imagine that there is no such thing as absolute truth is essentially a corruption of the hope we have in Christ. When Jesus said in John 14:6 that He is *the* way, *the* truth, and *the* life, He gave a fairly strong indication that there were absolutes in the world and that He is *the* standard. No wonder the Christian community suffers from the symptoms of a chronic loss of hope. Where hope is anchored in the quicksand of relativism, it has the sustaining power of warm Jell-O.

### The Authors of Hope

The second observation of the rising Christian battle with hopelessness has to do with our forfeit of our guide to hope—the Scriptures. If the hopelessness vaccine is fashioned from the cells of those who have looked into the face of hopelessness and defeated it, the Scriptures provide us with a limitless spiritual pharmacy of hope. If believers are to stand against a tide of hopelessness, we only need to open God's medicine cabinet and give ourselves regular injections.

Many of the men and women who pass through the pages of the Scriptures, tested and tormented, facing hardship and pain, suffering the full force of the storms of life, repeat as one their unshakable confidence in the ultimate refuge—God alone.

THE HOPE OF JOB. Consider the character of the hope of a man named Job. After facing immeasurable tragedy; losing all of his possessions, all of his children, and all of his friends, he expressed his confident hope this way:

> *"Though he slay me,* yet will I hope in him;
> *I will surely defend my ways to his face."*[19]

THE HOPE OF DAVID. David, the man after God's own heart, whose friend and king turned against him, who faced countless enemies from within and without, whose personal choices often left him grieving and humbled, left no doubt where his hope was found:

> *No king is saved by the size of his army;*
> *no warrior escapes by his great strength.*
> *A horse is a vain hope for deliverance;*
> *despite all its great strength it cannot save.*

> *But the eyes of the LORD*
> *are on those who fear him,*
> on those whose hope is in his unfailing love,
> *to deliver them from death*
> *and keep them alive in famine.*
> We wait in hope *for the LORD;*
> *he is our help and our shield.*[20]

THE HOPE OF ISAIAH. The prophet Isaiah, who faced ridicule and strife from the very people he came to serve, who lived a prophet's life of hardship and sacrifice, poetically described the unmistakable source of his hope:

> *Do you not know? Have you not heard?*
> *The LORD is the everlasting God,*
> *the Creator of the ends of the earth.*
> *He will not grow tired or weary,*
> *and his understanding no one can fathom.*
> *He gives strength to the weary*
> *and increases the power of the weak.*
> *Even youths grow tired and weary,*
> *and young men stumble and fall;*
> but those who hope in the LORD
> *will renew their strength.*
> *They will soar on wings like eagles;*
> *they will run and not grow weary,*
> *they will walk and not be faint.*[21]

THE HOPE OF JEREMIAH. The weeping prophet, Jeremiah, whom God called to watch the destruction and exile of his own people, knew where his hope came from:

> *"Do any of the worthless idols*
> *of the nations bring rain?*
> *Do the skies themselves send down showers?*
> *No, it is you, O LORD our God.*
> *Therefore our hope is in you,*
> *for you are the one who does all this."*[22]

THE HOPE OF PETER. Consider Peter, the man who walked with Christ on the land and on the water. The man whose denial of Christ echoes painfully from his day to ours lived to stand boldly in the courts and cities of his day and proclaim the message of the Resurrection, knowing where his hope came from:

> *For you know that it was not with perishable things such as silver or gold that you were redeemed from the empty way of life handed down to you from your forefathers, but with the precious blood of Christ, a lamb without blemish or defect. He was chosen before the creation of the world, but was revealed in these last times for your sake. Through him you believe in God, who raised him from the dead and glorified him, and* so your faith and hope are in God.[23]

THE HOPE OF PAUL. Which brings us to Paul, the apostle born out of season. The apostle of shipwrecks and stonings, of hardships and heartaches. The missionary apostle, pastor, and founder of churches. The Apostle of Hope. Paul's epistle to the Romans, particularly its eighth chapter, is perhaps the greatest treatise in all of written literature on the subject of hope. There is no mistaking the source of his hope. Therefore, we make it the road map for our present study:

> *We know that the whole creation has been groaning as in the pains of childbirth right up to the present time. Not only so, but we ourselves, who have the firstfruits of the Spirit, groan inwardly as we wait eagerly for our adoption as sons, the redemption of our bodies. For in this hope we were saved. But hope that is seen is no hope at all. Who hopes for what he already has? But if we hope for what we do not yet have, we wait for it patiently.*[24]

## THE HOPE OF MANKIND

I am not certain why my young friend decided to end his life that evening in his living room. I don't know exactly what it was on the horizon of his life that convinced him suicide was better than trying to make it through one more day. Why was the tomorrow he never saw that much more difficult than the countless yesterdays he had been through? I can't say. The depth of confusion and pain that compels someone to make this selfish, irreversible choice may be unfathomable.

I may not know his reason, but I know it did not have to be. This young man grew up in our church. He studied the Bible. He knew where to find hope. The tragedy of his death is all the more acute because he was unable to find his way to the one who could have given him all the hope he needed to carry him through.

I know that genuine hope can prevail in any struggle. I know that God is weaving the fabric of our lives with a purpose, even when the threads seem tangled to the point of ruin. I know that this kind of hope is available to anyone who wants it.

But I also know that this hope requires affirmation and validation. For our hope to remain strong, we must cultivate it, nurture it, and spread it around. We must draw from the well of God's Word and drink often, lest our hope dry up. We must exercise our hope, lest it atrophy and grow weak. And we must remember that the Source of our hope is always available and ever eager to replenish our supply.

# OUR HOPE

## SETS US FREE

# The Thief
# of Hope

*Therefore,*
*there is now no condemnation*
*for those who are in Christ Jesus,*
*because through Christ Jesus*
*the law of the Spirit of life*
*set me free from the law of sin and death.*

Romans 8:1-2

You need not know an RBI from an ERA to know that Mickey Mantle was a baseball player. His name alone sounds like it belongs to a baseball player. Like "Babe Ruth," it just fits. It sounds like baseball—the crack of a bat and the slap of a ball into a glove. Mickey Mantle, "the Mick." His name was so good that some people thought that he made it up. It was too good to be true, just as he was. But his name, along with his boyish good looks and amazing speed, was a gift. He was blessed with it as if it was a sacred trust—as if it was not just a name, but a destiny.

Sports reporter and lifelong baseball fan Bob Costas once said, "Mickey Mantle was the most compelling baseball hero of our time. . . . More than that, he was a presence in our lives. . . . He was *our* guy." "Mickey Mantle," Costas remembered, "*was* baseball."[1]

After 2,401 games played over eighteen seasons, he accumulated a lifetime .298 batting average, 536 home runs, 1,509 runs batted in, and 1,734 bases on balls—all in the process of winning baseball's Triple Crown once[2] and his league's Most Valuable Player award three times (in 1956, 1957, and 1962). On top of all that, he made twelve World Series appearances in his first fourteen seasons, and he was a member of seven world championship teams.

Costas spoke of Mantle with reverence as he remembered how "we creased our caps like him, we knelt down in an imaginary on-deck circle like him, and we ran like him—heads down, elbows up."[3] For a generation of young boys, Mickey Mantle was *the guy*.

According to Roger Angell, one of America's premier baseball writers, "You watched Willie [Mays] play, and you laughed all the time because he made it look fun. With Mantle, you didn't laugh. You gasped."[4]

He was the talented winner every kid wanted to be like. He was the hero that two decades of young boys looked up to. We may pull for the underdogs, but when a generation of young boys stared down fast balls at the home plates of sandlots all over America, it was number 7 they pretended to be. Mickey Mantle was an American original and an American immortal.

God had given Mickey Mantle something special, a gift afforded very few. Anyone with even a casual interest in baseball and a slight belief in a Creator would say that Mickey Charles Mantle was special, that he had the fingerprints of God on his life.

### SMUDGING THE FINGERPRINTS OF GOD

You could also say that Mickey Mantle spent the better part of his life smudging those fingerprints. Even though many people think of him as the greatest baseball player since World War II, most admit that he could have been even better.

When Casey Stengel, Mantle's manager for almost ten years, left him off his "All-Time Team," sportswriters said that Stengel seemed to be punishing Mantle for not living up to his destiny. Mickey himself freely admitted he had wasted the talent God had given him. "Everybody tries to make the excuse that injuries shortened my career. Truth is . . . the doctors would give me rehab work to do, and I wouldn't do it. I'd be out drinking."[5] He was great, but he knew he could have been even greater. The true greatness that seemed to be his destiny slipped through his fingers. In the end, even he knew he had squandered a rare treasure.

On June 1, 1995, Mickey Mantle entered Baylor Hospital in Dallas. All of the privilege and fame, all of the strength and skill, all of the success and adulation were tinged with regret and sorrow during the press conference Mantle held after receiving a liver transplant on June 8, 1995. He bluntly admitted he had spent his life abusing his blessings. He candidly told how he had squandered his skills, neglected his family, and mismanaged his good fortune.

But Mickey Mantle has a lot of company in smudging God's fingerprints. Most of us have made that mistake at one time or another.

Have you ever wrestled with your own stupidity and lost?

Have you ever continued to punish yourself for not saying or doing the right thing long after you could do anything about it?

Do you hang on to regrets from times when you spent instead of saved? Indulged instead of refrained?

Long after the dust has settled and the smoke has cleared, do you find yourself struggling with your past?

## REGRET: THE THIEF OF HOPE

What do you regret about your life?

What are your disappointments?

Do memories of failures and missed opportunities cloud your view of the past?

Do "I wish I would've . . ." "If only I'd . . ." "I know I could've . . ." play like top forty tunes in your head?

Does "How could I have been so stupid?" or "What on earth was I thinking?" sound familiar?

Join the club. These are the lyrics of regret, and most of us know the tune.

### The Reality of Regret

We all live with some regrets. Unwise decisions, stupid choices, failures, disappointments, and mistakes make up the fabric of all of our lives. If I compiled a list of all the boneheaded and/or idiotic decisions

I have made in my life, it would easily fill multiple volumes in the encyclopedia of stupidity.

There are some things in our lives that we cannot, and perhaps should not, ever forget. The consequences to some of the choices we have made we may never escape. There are bad—sometimes terrible—things that have happened to us outside of our control that we will live with the rest of our lives. The tuition charged by the school of hard knocks is too high for us to forget the lessons learned there. But there is an important difference between learning from our mistakes and living in regret.

I have sat with couples trying to survive unfaithfulness, dishonesty, and tragedy. I have wept with abandoned wives and listened to the grief caused by rebellious teenagers. I have felt the blow of decisions that have ended relationships and destroyed families. And I have seen the great harm resulting when these wounds fester with unforgiveness, revenge, and guilt. Having seen so many casualties from the battle to do what is right, I have to believe that God has a plan of restoration and hope.

Regret is real. Failure happens. Mistakes hurt. Sorrow and guilt can shadow our lives for any length of time. But God does have a plan. The light of forgiveness and freedom can shine even in the darkest struggles of life. Regret may wound us, but it does not have to destroy us. We may be struggling, but we do not have to be defeated. The way may be dark, but there is a light. It is the light of hope.

### The Lyrics of Regret

In the seventh chapter of the book of Romans, the apostle Paul sings the popular tune of regret, a song I find all too familiar. The book of Romans is considered by many to be the greatest theological work in the New Testament. It provides an elegant, concise *basis for what a Christian is to believe* and the *basics for how a Christian is to behave*. In the first eleven chapters, man's need and God's plan are majestically outlined with unparalleled supernatural depth. The unfolding drama of redemption is spelled out so vividly that this one book has been used by God to literally change the course of human history.

Yet in the seventh chapter of this book, in what we might say is one of the most "spiritual" books ever written, Paul candidly confesses to the most human of struggles. In this pious context, with this holy subject, the inspired writer confesses that he "blows it."

All of the exegetical gymnastics designed to "explain" this confession cannot blunt its impact. All of the pious varnish possible cannot hide the knotholes. All of the sanctimonious shushing from the holiest of interpreters cannot silence the ruckus raised by Paul's wrestling with his conscience in the living room of our lives.

Those of us who struggle with regret, disappointment, and disobedience may also consider this to be one of the most encouraging revelations in the entire Bible. In this passage, Paul takes his place alongside the arrogant Abraham, the cowardly Moses, the lustful David, the frightened Elijah, the hypocritical Peter, the doubting Thomas, and real-life believers—us.

Our theology by experience tells us that even though we love God and hate sin, it is a battle to behave the way we should. The question of our righteousness is certainly settled in heaven, but our struggle with unrighteousness rears its ugly head in our lives every day. Paul knew this struggle as well as anyone, and it is encouraging to know that he knew.

Romans 8 opens with the word *therefore*. This indicates that what follows is to be understood in light of what was said before. And to put it in a simplistic vernacular, what was said before in Romans 7:14-25 was: "I blow it. I know what it means to struggle with sin." But what comes next, Romans 8, is the rest of the story.

## HOPE IN 3-D

Last week I sat down with a large group of people from our church for a discussion on the subject of hope. For over an hour we analyzed it, theorized about it, and tried to define it. Not surprisingly, we could not do it to everyone's satisfaction. We considered numerous passages from the Bible. We exegeted our experiences and shared our opinions, but still found it difficult to get our minds around the concept of hope. One person came up to me afterward and said, "Thanks. Now I'm more confused than when we started." Another person added, "I'm leaving with more questions than answers. I *hope* [spoken with that sarcastic intonation that indicates a significant play on words is taking place and it would be best to chuckle appropriately[6]] we can figure hope out."

## Hope Speak

The idea of hope, or some form of it, is very familiar to us. However, apart from the nominative references to Bob Hope or President Clinton's hometown of Hope, Arkansas, we have a hard time pinning down exactly what hope is. Yet "hope speak" perforates our speech in defiance of our unfamiliarity with its nature.

We hope to see people soon.

We hope they get well, have a nice day, have a safe trip, or that they are right about that weather forecast.

We are hopeful, hoping, hopeless, or as my mother used to tell me, beyond all hope.

We can hope against hope when there is little or no hope.

We can hope in hope when we have nothing but hope.

We can get more than we hoped for and hope for more than we get.

We can give hope as long as we don't give up hope.

We hope for the best and hang on to our best hopes.

We have been told to keep hope alive, to share hope, bring hope, find hope, and have hope.

We hope you don't mind.

We hope you understand.

We hope and hope and hope.

I hope you get the point.

## Hope's Future Dimension

Along with faith and love, hope forms the third fundamental pillar of the Christian life. Hope is as important to the believer as both love and faith, and it is just as deep. In order to form a framework for our understanding of hope, not to limit its scope but to "flesh it out," I want to suggest that hope, as described in Romans 8, has three dimensions—a past, a present, and a future.

We often focus on the eschatological or the future dimension of hope. This is how dictionaries most often define hope—in terms of a desire, a wish, an expectation, or an anticipation. The future dimension of hope is very important to the believer.

In fact, the eschatological dimension of hope is the great hope of the Bible. The future reign of the King of Kings and Lord of Lords, the day when every knee shall bow and every tongue confess that Jesus Christ is Lord, is the day upon which all our future hopes are fixed. Christians in the midst of the trials of life can endure only if they will focus clearly on the day when all things will be made new, made known, and made right. This promise of a hope still future sustains us through the injustices and inexplicable trials of this life. It is the hope of heaven.

### Hope's Present Condition

The present dimension of hope we understand less precisely. But when we are encouraged to find our hope in His Word, and the one who hopes in the Lord is commended, we see the dimension of a living and practical hope. Having hope should have an effect on the way we live. We can have hope for a day yet to come and still find hope in the day that is here.

A hope that has no place in our daily lives means that we become, as the saying goes, "so heavenly minded that we are of no earthly good." The present dimension of hope is hope in action. To better understand hope, we should look for signs of it in our lives and ministries today.

### Hope's Past Foundation

The past dimension of hope is perhaps the least familiar, yet in some ways, the most important. The past dimension of hope forms the foundation for our hope. If we have no hope of forgiveness, if our lives are riddled with regret, if we have no hope of freedom from guilt and grief, then we do not understand the hope we have in Christ. The past dimension is what we hope *in*, not what we hope *for*.

Romans 8 provides us with an opportunity to consider all three dimensions of hope. We can learn more about the future dimension of hope as we consider 8:28-39. We can learn more about the present dimension of hope as we consider 8:12-27. And we can begin where Romans 8 does, by considering the past dimension of our hope in 8:1-11.

Romans 8 begins with a perspective of hope built upon the foundation of a past that is forgiven. The connection between the struggles of Romans 7 and the hope of Romans 8 is not accidental nor incidental. In Romans 7 we realize that we are not making the headway we think we should. We should be faster, stronger, better. We tripped and fell, and as far as we know, the rest of the race is going to be no better. There is no hope for us. We are screw-ups. We are losers. Romans 8 however, picks us up, dusts us off, and places our feet on a path of hope.

## THE FOUNDATION OF FORGIVENESS

The first two verses of Romans 8 provide a rock-solid foundation for the hope upon which we can build our lives. A life built on this foundation provides us with a reason not to throw in the towel, not to hang our heads, and not to quit the race. The foundation stone is simple and yet profound: It is the forgiveness we have in Christ. *"Therefore, there is now no condemnation for those who are in Christ Jesus."*

The actual first word in the Greek text is emphatic, not only because of its priority in the sentence, but also in its meaning. In this case, *therefore* is not the first word of this sentence; no οὐδέν (*ouden*) is. This word means more than a simple no; it literally means "no, not even one, none." To say it as emphatically as possible: There is not one single possible condemnation—none, *nada,* zero, zippo, zilch, *nunca,* goose egg, doughnut hole, Cheerios zero—absolutely, positively none. The grace and mercy of God given to us in Christ are so much greater than all of our sin that no condemnation possible can black it out.

When the shadow of regret falls on our lives, when the struggles and trials of life darken our path, when the pain of memories and the grief over what might have been cause us to give up hope, the first words of Romans 8 rekindle our hope. The darkest moments will never blot out the light of His forgiveness—for there is no condemnation—none, *nada,* zero, zippo.

## GUILTY BUT UNCONDEMNED

To reinforce the foundation of our forgiveness, the apostle continues to construct his argument like a skilled mason, laying the foundation block by block. He places next in his foundation a carefully chosen word—*condemnation.*

The word for condemnation, κατάκριμα (*katakrima*), is a word Paul uses only three times in all of his writings (in Rom. 5:16, 18, and 8:1). In fact, it is used only these three times in the entire New Testament. It is a forensic or legal term that focuses on the result of a judgment. The most descriptive term we have like it is *doom,* or perhaps more specifically, *sentence* or *punishment.*

By implication then, we realize the strength of the connection between our mistakes and God's forgiveness. Romans 8:1 does not teach us that our actions do not have consequences or that obedience is unimportant. We are not free from the struggle to do what is right, nor are we unaccountable for our choices. But we can be certain that the penalty for our sin, the "doom" that comes upon those who are disobedient, we will have no part of—none, *nada,* zero, zip. Metaphorically speaking, we may face the trial, but we will never face the final punishment.

## LIVIN' FORGIVEN

This deliverance from doom, however, is not unconditional. There is only one way to make certain that this mercy will be shown for every mistake, will cover every sin, will be applied to every conviction. This mercy is tied to the final phrase of verse one: *"for those who are in Christ Jesus."* The key word here is the one that is easiest to overlook—*in.*

In order for this forgiveness to be applied, you have to be *"in"* Christ Jesus. This means more than simply to be *"with"* Him. It is not simply an awareness that He is or even of who He is. It is not simply an acquaintance with Him or being able to identify Him. It means *to be a part of Him.* The Bible makes it very plain that to be "in" Christ requires one commitment—a commitment of faith. To be in Christ means to believe that He is the Savior you need and to place your faith in Him.

When we blow it, when we are guilty as charged, when we have every reason to give up hope, we need not. Our hope rests not on the perfection of our character, but upon the perfect quality of forgiveness in Christ. When the shadow of regret and failure grows long across our lives, the light of hope still shines. We may be guilty, but we are not condemned.

## THE FOUNDATION OF FREEDOM

Alcatraz is a twenty-two-acre island in the middle of the San Francisco Bay, one and a half miles from the closest shoreline. This rocky fortress served from 1934 to 1963 as one of the most notorious maximum-security prisons in America. Though some have claimed otherwise, officially no one has ever successfully escaped from "The Rock."

If Alcatraz was an impregnable fortress, then the book of Romans tells us that our sinful nature is our own personal Alcatraz. This prison does not require concrete walls and bars to hold us. Razor wire and guard dogs are not necessary to incarcerate us. Our fallen, rebellious, disobedient natures imprison us far more effectively.

### THE GREAT ESCAPE

For much of the early part of Paul's letter to the Romans, he makes it clear that the Law, God's Old Testament Law, was given by God to both con-vict us of our disobedience and to reveal to us our imprisoned condition. But as Paul personally expresses in Romans 7, the Law is incapable of set-ting us free. We are unable to escape from this prison on our own, and the Law of God was never designed to get us out. As Paul cries out in Romans 7:24, *"What a wretched man I am! Who will rescue me from this body of death?"*

However, just a few verses later in Romans 8:2, we are given the key to the prison: *"because through Christ Jesus the law of the Spirit of life set me free from the law of sin and death."* In a jailbreak of eternal proportions, we go from facing life in prison one moment to finding freedom the next. Once slaves with no future, condemned to life under a cruel master, we are all at once let go, set free.

Charles Wesley expressed this profound, amazing transformation in the words of his hymn "And Can It Be That I Should Gain":

> *Long my imprisoned spirit lay*
> *Fast bound in sin and nature's night.*
> *Thine eye diffused a quick'ning ray:*
> *I woke, the dungeon flamed with light!*
> *My chains fell off, my heart was free,*
> *I rose, went forth, and followed Thee.*

We were once locked away without the possibility of escape or parole. The chains of all of our regrets and mistakes were fastened tightly around our ankles. Our incarceration was secured with a lock for which there was no key. We were truly hopeless. But not anymore.

## The Alcatraz of Hope

We live in a hypocritical world that on the one hand aggressively denies the reality of this prison while on the other hand desperately seeking a way of escape. If we look closely at our culture, we find people tunneling for freedom, digging themselves into ever deeper holes—financial holes, relational holes, behavioral holes. We find people plotting their escape from the prison of pain through science, technology, psychology, and philosophy.

We find people surrendering to the hopelessness, denying that the walls even exist and simply living for as much momentary pleasure as possible. They may be building their castles, but these are mansions built within the walls of the fortress. Despite their wealth, these people do not know freedom.

Perhaps we forget or never even realized how hopeless the situation really is apart from Jesus Christ: Memories that never fade. Wounds that never heal. Scars that never go away. Living as slaves to our own needs, desires, and insatiable appetites. Collecting trophies and treasures that never seem to be enough. Always pursuing but never attaining. Seeking and never finding. Surrounded by many and yet always alone. Unable to escape. Without the hope of real freedom.

### Hope Written in the Dust

There once was a woman who in one terrifying afternoon came to realize her brutal, unmerciful imprisonment. Though we don't know much about her, we know something of people like her. As it turns out, she perhaps was not all that different from you and me.

We can imagine that she would not stand out in a crowd. She possibly had a husband and perhaps children. She could easily have had a group of friends—other women who were raising families and caring for their husbands as she was. We can imagine her visiting the marketplace, washing clothes, mending garments, and making a home. She could have been known as a sister or a cousin, an aunt or a daughter, a wife or a mom. We know very little of the details of her life except one: We know the details of the day she came to realize, perhaps without warning, that she was a prisoner.

LOCKED IN A PRISON OF PASSION. She was a prisoner of her passions, a slave to her desires. We do not know whether there was an ache within her for love, a void left by an abusive father or an inattentive husband. We cannot know for certain if she was overwhelmed by feelings of loneliness, inadequacy, or self-doubt. It is possible that she was searching desperately for some happiness or a momentary escape. Perhaps she was compelled by a deep longing for attention. We know nothing of the story written on her heart. We only know that she was a slave, a prisoner, unable to say no.

It is quite possible that on the day her life was changed, she was being used by others in their self-serving schemes. It is possible that she was actually an unwilling victim of a grand conspiracy. We don't know for sure, but it doesn't really matter. On that day she came to realize clearly that she was a prisoner. The events of that day set her free.

A group of men burst in on her, and she was, to say the least, unprepared to go with them. In fact she was unprepared to go anywhere or to be seen publicly by anyone. To say that they found her in a humiliating and compromising position is a cruel understatement. The men had come upon her when she least expected it, as she was in the secret embrace of her lover. She had been caught indulging her passion in the arms of a man who was not her husband.

Her humiliation would have turned to fear as her pious captors dragged her into the street, parading her publicly through the city. Her compromised condition would have been evident to everyone as they passed by. Her confusion and shame would have been equaled only by her fear of what was yet to come.

THE WAY OF ESCAPE. The men dragged her through the streets and into the temple. It was there that they threw her at the feet of their theological nemesis, Jesus of Nazareth. He had come into Jerusalem at dawn that day and was teaching in the temple courts, the most public place in all Jerusalem. While it was customary for teaching and debate to take place along the walls of Herod's great temple, we can be certain that no one had ever taught within those temple walls as Jesus did.

He could describe, as no one before or since, what God saw as He watched the activity there. He was able to tell the gathering crowds incredible stories of King David's passion for God and lifelong desire to build a temple such as this. He could describe in detail the struggle in raising Herod's splendid temple.

Jesus was the only person in history who could tell personally and with great empathetic passion of the grief of Jeremiah in witnessing its destruction. With the objectivity of an eyewitness and the subjectivity of a loving father, Jesus could teach unlike anyone else. The crowds around him that day would have certainly been enormous.

Those who opposed Jesus' teaching forced their way toward Him, their adulterous prize in hand. Interrupting Him, they threw her before Jesus and the crowd to trumpet her sin. These men were experts in the Law, legal and theological professionals. They knew exactly what they were doing. They spoke boldly as they reminded Jesus before all those gathered in the temple courts that the Law of Moses demanded that this woman be put to death. They quoted chapter and verse: An adulteress was to be taken from the city, bound, and placed in the midst of the people, who would then take up stones and bludgeon her to death.

These legal experts obviously knew of Jesus' compassion. They had apparently heard of His teaching on forgiveness. They also knew that if He was in fact a teacher of the Law, He must be willing to follow its instructions to the letter. If He let her go, He would be a false teacher. If He joined in her stoning, His message of compassion and forgiveness would be hypocritical. His position seemed as hopeless as the woman who stood before Him.

IN HIS PRESENCE. Without being irresponsible, I like to think that at this moment Jesus' eyes met the woman's. I like to imagine that this woman, clutching desperately at her garments to sustain what little modesty she had left, her face streaked with dirt and tears, her hair knotted and disheveled, caught his wordless gaze and, in an instant, felt safe. As she stood trembling with fear before her captors and the nameless spectators, it is possible that Jesus could have comforted her simply by His presence and the power of His demeanor, much like a father casting a shadow over his child. I can't prove this; the text offers no indication that the woman looked at Jesus or even knew who He was—but she was about to know.

As the woman stood before her accusers, John 8:6 tells us that Jesus bent down and began writing in the dirt with His finger. Again the text does not tell us what He wrote. It may have been a brief, simple word to confound the men. He may have written a list of words, perhaps even a list of their private sins. He may have written their names or the names of their adulterous lovers. We don't know. But when the legal experts and the religious leaders demanded that Jesus respond to their questions, He simply told them what the Law required—to stone her. But He said that any one of them who was without sin should be the first one to cast a stone. Then he went back to writing in the dirt.

The moment must have been filled with silence as the first of the legal scholars turned and made his escape through the crowd. As another turned to leave, and then another, Jesus simply kept writing in the dirt, saying nothing. We do not know what happened to the crowd that had gathered to hear Jesus teach, but I know that if I were there, I would have stayed. I would have been pushing my way to the front to see what was going on. I would have wanted to know what He was writing on the ground. I would have wanted to hear what Jesus was going to say to this woman.

After 2,000 years, those words in the dirt have been wiped into obscurity. However, we can still hear what Jesus said to this woman. For all that we don't know about this story, we do know that. Jesus asked where her accusers were. He asked her if there was no one left to cast a stone at her.

It is not hard to imagine the woman's hair hanging like a veil over her face, her head bowed, her tear-filled eyes unwilling to look up at Jesus' face, the tears falling among the words Jesus had written in the dirt.

Between the sobs her response was humble and quiet: *"No one, sir."* In her response we recognize her understanding of Jesus' forgiveness, for He was still standing with her. Even as the two stood alone in the crowd, even though Jesus had mentioned nothing of His intentions, the woman trusted in His forgiveness.

With that, I see Jesus reaching out and lifting her chin so that she would look into His face as He said, *"Then neither do I condemn you."* Jesus spoke loudly enough for those remaining to hear. *"Go now, and leave your life of sin."* And with those words, He set her free.

### Sinners Set Free

Many lessons are woven into this story—lessons of forgiveness, judgment, mercy, and grace. Even though this passage is of questionable textual credibility, we are drawn to its lessons, for they seem so classic in their portrait of our Savior.

But the lesson for us considering the subject of hope and the text of Romans 8:2 is the lesson of freedom. Jesus' words to the adulterous woman personalize the truth of Romans 8:2. By His grace, through His mercy, because of His forgiveness, this woman was set free. She was free not to sin anymore.

What Romans 8:2 teaches us is that by the power of the Spirit of God, we are free *not* to sin. The law of sin and death, the power that gave us no choice but to sin, has been superseded by the law of the Spirit of life.

The principle of Romans 8:2 is not that we are set free and never will sin again. Romans 7:14-25 reminds us, along with our own experience, that this is not the freedom we have. As long as we are imprisoned in this Alcatraz of flesh, in our natural bodies, we will struggle with our natural desires. But unlike those who are not in Christ, we no longer *have* to sin. We now have an option *not* to sin.

### Escape from The Rock

While Alcatraz was virtually escape-proof, many men were freed from there. A pardon or the payment of their debt to society was the only hope of a man locked away in Alcatraz. So too our hope is found in the pardon and the payment of our debt by Jesus Christ. There is only one way out, and it is through Him. It is the law of the Spirit of life that sets us free.

When we grow weary in the struggle to do the right thing, when we become overwhelmed by the trauma and trials of life, when we are standing in the shadows of our own mistakes and failures, we may think we have imprisoned ourselves in a jail of our own stupidity without hope of escape. But we have a hope for release based not on ourselves, but on the person and work of Jesus Christ. No matter how often or how badly we fail, our freedom and our hope rests on solid rock. And on this alone.

## HOPE'S HOME RUN

Mickey Mantle told *Sports Illustrated* in an interview about a year before his death, "[My manager] Casey [Stengel] said, 'This guy's going to be better than DiMaggio.' It didn't happen. God gave me a great body, and I didn't take care of it."[7]

If anyone understood regret, it was Mickey Charles Mantle. In the convergence of talent and opportunity, he had it all. But it was a talent poured out in a self-destructive lifestyle, potential washed away in a sea of alcohol, expectations of greatness drowned. But this is not the end of the story.

One week after Mickey Mantle was hospitalized in Dallas on June 1, 1995, the press stated that Mantle was suffering from liver cancer. He would need a liver transplant operation to survive.

On Wednesday afternoon, August 9, 1995, Mickey Mantle's family friend and attorney, Roy True, called Mickey's former teammate, long-time friend and Christian, Bobby Richardson, who was living in South Carolina. True told him that Mickey was not doing well, and he asked if Bobby and his wife would make the trip to Dallas to visit with Mickey. Bobby and his wife, Betsy, arrived in Dallas that evening.

The next morning Bobby went alone to Baylor Hospital in Dallas.

Mickey was visiting with Yankee teammate Whitey Ford when Richardson arrived. As Ford left the room, Mantle was perked up by his meeting with Whitey, and he noticed Richardson standing in the back of the room. Mickey excitedly asked Bobby to come close.

It was Richardson's understanding—though he could not be specific—that Mantle's doctors had "leveled with him" about his condition and that he knew he was going to die. "What he didn't know was when—and he didn't want to know," Richardson said.[8]

"Bobby, I've been wanting to tell you something," Mickey said.
"What's that?" Bobby asked, drawing near the bed.
"I want you to know that I have accepted Christ," Mickey told Bobby. On hearing this, Richardson began to weep. Then he prayed with Mickey and shared an intimacy that only two brothers in Christ can have. The angels in heaven, not the ones in California, were cheering. It was Mantle's longest home run.

Following their prayer, Bobby said to Mickey, "I just want to make sure, Mick." And with that he rehearsed again the plan of salvation.

As Richardson concluded the plan of salvation, Mickey looked at Bobby and said plainly, "That's what I've done."

Four days later, in the early hours of Sunday, August 13, Mickey Mantle went home for the last time. In a life filled with glory and great moments, this was certainly the greatest and most glorious victory.

Once again Mickey Mantle knows the blessing of the hand of God. But now the fingerprints cannot be smudged—for the ultimate blessing of God is the freedom of forgiveness. All of the regrets, all of the mistakes, and all of the pain have been washed away. Mickey is free, safe at home.

If we understand what the Bible means by hope, we understand that no matter how many regrets we have in our lives, no matter how many failures, no matter how many disappointments, there is a Savior who forgives us and sets us free, that there is, in fact, not one bit of condemnation for those who are in Christ Jesus. We then understand how we can have hope even when we ourselves smudge His fingerprints.

For in the shadow of our regret shines the brightest light—
His hope.

# The Hero
# of Hope

*For what the law was powerless to do*
  *in that it was weakened by the sinful nature,*
  *God did by sending his own Son*
  *in the likeness of sinful man*
  *to be a sin offering.*
*And so he condemned sin in sinful man,*
  *in order that the righteous requirements of the law*
  *might be fully met in us,*
  *who do not live according to the sinful nature*
  *but according to the Spirit.*

*Romans 8:3-4*

"We've had a Main Bus B undervolt" may sound like nonsensical engineering gibberish to most of us. In fact, this spurt of scientific techno-babble is meaningless to anyone without the background to understand its grave implications. But at precisely 9:07 P.M., Central Standard Time, on April 13, 1970, an army of people fluent in such techno-speak all quickly knew that this gibberish meant serious trouble.

The problem threatened the lives of three men over 200,000 miles from home and heading farther away at a speed of seven miles per second. These three men, as a result of their "Main Bus B undervolt," were clinging to life in the unforgiving void of outer space. They would now require all of the intelligence, skills, and talents of this army of scientists if they were ever to get back home alive. For the next four days every resource would be sacrificially devoted to the rescue of these three men.

The men of Apollo 13.

## LOST IN SPACE

James Lovell, Fred Haise, and Jack Swigert were well on their way to being the third team of men in human history to set foot on the moon. Just fifty-six hours after liftoff, their spacecraft—the only thing separating them from the deadly vacuum of space and the only means of sustaining their lives—suffered a catastrophic malfunction.

An explosion ten feet behind their seats in the number 2 cryogenic oxygen tank wiped out most of their supply of air, electricity, and water. They were 80 percent of the way to the moon, almost 220,000 miles from home, and they were venting their supply of oxygen out into the void of outer space faster than they were breathing it. Without a near-miraculous rescue, these three men were minutes away from becoming lifeless space debris.

### Miles from Home, Inches from Death

Imagine how it feels to suddenly realize that most of your supply of breathable air has just leaked out into the void of space and that the only source of more breathable air in the known universe is 200,000 miles in the opposite direction.

In addition, you must also remember that in order to stay alive, you must make a journey in a crippled spacecraft of roughly *half a million* miles. And that while you are on this journey back to your wonderful blue home planet, any miscalculation in terms of inches, decimal places, or portions of seconds could send you skipping off the beautiful blue Earth's precious atmosphere and propel you helplessly into an interstellar oblivion.

It is less than hope-inspiring to understand not only that you might soon run out of air to breathe, but also that you might forget to carry a number in your math, and with that one mistake wind up in an orbital eternity.

### Never Alone

How is it possible that under such disastrous conditions these men kept up their hope?

Were they so courageous that giving up never crossed their minds?

Were they so confident in their own skills and training that to lose hope never occurred to them?

Were they so disciplined that to quit trying was never a temptation?

How could they have been so rational? So calm? So hopeful?

The thin thread of hope that pulled the crew of Apollo 13 back to earth could be found in the confidence they had in the technicians, scientists, engineers, and astronauts devoted to bringing them back alive. The hope of Apollo 13's safe return rested upon the enormous sacrifice of the people at NASA, the Draper Institute at MIT, Grumman Aerospace, and other people around the world sacrificially working toward their rescue.

## MISSION CONTROL

During the Apollo space flights, Mission Control in Houston was staffed by four teams of the best scientists, engineers, and technicians in the world. In less than ten years they had overseen the evolution of manned space flight from the vapor of a mere dream, through the Mercury and Gemini missions, to the reality of placing a man on the moon. Along with the countless developers, contractors, designers, and others who built the spacecraft, this group was the best in the world at what they did.

In the hours and days following the crippling of Apollo 13, this group of people came together to form one of the most impressive brain trusts ever assembled in the history of space flight. If there was a reason above any other reason not to give up hope, it was based upon the work of this small, dedicated group, the only ones in the world who could do what they did.

### Living in a Crippled Ship

Most of us do not consider our lives to be in similar peril. We are not 200,000 miles from Earth with two thin layers of steel between us and a deadly vacuum, heading away from home at an astounding rate of speed in a severely crippled ship.

Maybe we should reconsider.

Perhaps our "data" does not inform us of immediate danger. Possibly, we have been sailing comfortably through life, no recent explosions rocking our ship. We have no sense that we are inches away from fatality or moments away from disaster.

But does this really mean, metaphorically speaking, that we are not lost in space?

Just because the trip has been smooth so far, does that absolutely reassure us that we are not heading at an incredible rate of speed *in the wrong direction*?

Just because our lives are not in imminent danger, does that mean we are secure?

Or could our own ship be as fragile as that of Apollo 13?

On the other hand, you may realize all too well the frailty of your situation. You may not know a "Main Bus B undervolt" from a cross-town bus, but you certainly know what it means to face a crisis. You recognize only too well the sound of catastrophe. The shocks in your life are not coming from exploding cryogenic oxygen tanks, but from children's lives unraveling, jobs imploding, or relationships falling apart. There may be overwhelming grief, inexplicable tragedy, or financial catastrophe. As you look at your life, the metaphor of a crippled spacecraft on the brink of disaster seems to fit a little too well.

### The Mission Controller

The Apollo command module had over one million different systems. Just to monitor these systems required a team of hundreds. In a crisis like the one facing Apollo 13, hundreds more experts contributed their knowledge to solving the highly technical problems of survival. In our case, the staff of our Mission Control is more than adequately filled by the creator of our vessel—God the Father, the Mission Controller—Jesus Christ, and the in-flight supervisor—the Holy Spirit.

Mission Controller is an appropriate description of Jesus Christ. He is the designer, the technician, the expert, the master of all of the infinitely complicated systems of life. How incredible to think that Jesus Christ alone can oversee the flights not just of one individual or even one family, but the flights of all mankind.

If the crew of Apollo 13 found hope in knowing that the expertise, dedication, and sacrifice of the greatest scientists, engineers, designers, and technicians—the total support of countless talented people—were available to them, then shouldn't it be possible for us to find hope, even in the darkest of hours, from the creator, designer, and sustainer of *all the universe*?

When all is said and done, those of us who place our faith in Jesus Christ have but one source of genuine hope, and He is enough. And when we encounter danger on our journey, when the mission meets tragedy, and our homecoming is thrown into doubt, there is one we can call on to bring us home.

Romans 8:3-4 serves as a theological job description for Jesus Christ. He is more than qualified to sit where the Ph.D.s, professors, and experts sit in Mission Control. As a reminder of just how skillful and amazing He is, consider for a moment His two key qualifications as our chief flight controller. To have hope in times of disaster, just consider what we are told in Romans 8:3-4 about who Jesus is and what He has done.

## ALL THAT THE LAW COULD NOT DO,
### HE DID

The Law, as the young rabbinical scholar Saul studied it, contained far more than the Ten Commandments. The Law Saul studied was first of all comprised of the Torah, the writings of Moses. These writings, the Pentateuch, are the first five books of the Old Testament: Genesis, Exodus, Leviticus, Numbers, and Deuteronomy.

In addition to the hundreds of moral, judicial, and ritual commands of the Torah, the young rabbi would have also studied all of the historical, prophetic, and poetic writings of the Old Testament. He would have had to familiarize himself with the chronicles of Israel's history and prophetic future.

Finally, added to this volume of inspired writings and instructions was the Talmud. These were the collected writings from centuries of respected legal interpreters dating from about the time of Ezra (450 B.C.). While the Talmud is not technically a Spirit-breathed part of the Law contained in the Scriptures, it formed an important part of the study of a young rabbi.

## THE POWER OF THE LAW

By Paul's day, the Law and all that went with it amounted to the greatest socio-literary achievement in history. The Law served to guide and inform the people of God on every aspect of life from birth to death. To this day, there is nothing like it in the history of civilization.

Consider for a moment the life-changing power of just a fraction of the Law, the Ten Commandments. The Decalogue, or the "ten words," appears only twice in the writings of Moses (in Ex. 20:1-17 and Deut. 5:6-21). Yet these ten simple commands form the foundation for all of the rest of the Law.[1]

If we were to live in a nation built upon complete obedience to only these ten commands, we would instantly wipe out all crime and murder, selfishness and greed, adultery, divorce, dishonesty, and disrespect. At the same time, through simple adherence to just "ten words," we could establish obedience, humility, respect, and holiness. These ten simple commands are so transcendent of time and culture that they could be applied anywhere, at any period in history, to any people. If we had no other laws to live by, we could build a completely civilized society. This is the power of the Law.

In underscoring the surpassing greatness of Jesus Christ and His work in redemption, Paul is careful not to diminish the inspiration and power of the Law. This is difficult to do, for in the shadow of who Jesus Christ is and what He accomplished, everything else appears completely inadequate. But in Romans 8:3, we find Paul's inspired solution.

### The Inspired Solution

In this verse Paul states that God did what the Law *was powerless to do, in that it was weakened by sinful flesh.* With this statement he is demonstrating his respect and passion for the Law in two ways.

The first way is by what he does *not* say about the Law. He does not say that the Law was intrinsically impotent. The Law is in fact inspired and powerful. There is much that it can do. The Law has the ability to show people how to live. It has the ability to guide and guard a society, to build families and to create communities. The Law of God is so amazing that it even has the ability to reveal God's character. It has the ability to point people to God. The Law is "good." Paul does not say here that the Law could not do these good things.

Second, Paul demonstrates his passion for God's Law by affirming that it was not the Law that failed to perform as God designed it, but rather it was the sinful men and women trying to carry it out who failed. The Law was never designed to overcome our own "sin nature." The design wasn't at fault; the problem was with the sinful operators who never could apply it consistently enough for it to be effective.[2]

### Design Flaws

My brother-in-law builds and drives race cars. He has forgotten more about cars than I will ever know. One time I went with him to an autocross competition. We took a car that he had built himself, designed specifically for this kind of racing. It had roll bars, sway bars, torsion bars—and if you weren't careful driving it, you could wind up behind prison bars. He drove it so well that he was able to compete with other cars that had much greater horsepower and more sophisticated suspension technology. He was able to drive the car as it was designed to be driven—at its limit.

However, when I had the opportunity to drive the car, I could not match his performance. I drove like crazy, doing everything I could to drive it flat out, only to find that I was nowhere near as fast as my brother-in-law. Brakes squealed, tires skidded, and cones flew, but I was not able to, as racers say, "get everything out of the car."

Was this my brother-in-law's fault? Had he designed the car incorrectly? Was there something wrong with what he had done, or was the problem with me? The well-designed car only served to display my inadequacy as a race driver.

So it is with God's Law. It was never designed to fully make up for the inadequacies and iniquities of those who use it. It never had the ability to overcome our sinful nature. In fact, it was designed primarily to allow us to live as well as possible, while showing us that it is impossible to live perfectly apart from the grace of God. If the Law was inadequate, it was not by the hand of its Designer; it was so in the hands of its sinful operators.

### A Fan of the Latter

Paul, a fan of the former Law and a fan of the latter Son, goes on to communicate how amazing the accomplishments of the Son really are when he says in Romans 8:3, "*. . . God did by sending his own Son in the likeness of sinful man, to be a sin offering. And so he condemned sin in sinful man.*" As great as the Law was, the Son is greater. The Son did what the Law could not do: He overcame the inadequacies of the sinful man. Jesus Christ did what the Law was never designed to do—He overpowered sin.

Theologically speaking, this is the nature of substitutionary atonement: Jesus Christ condemned the sin that condemns us. In other words, He defeated sin so that it no longer could defeat us. This is not only something the Law could not do; it is something that only God's sinless Son could do.[3]

### A TALE OF TWO SONS

The story has been told of twin brothers growing up on the streets of Brooklyn, New York, at the turn of the century. These two boys, descendants of deposed royalty, grew up in the home of their hard-working but impoverished immigrant parents. While they were far from wealthy, they always had clothes on their backs, shoes on their feet, and food in their stomachs. They were very much like the other children in their neighborhood, unaware of their own poverty and content in their ignorance.

These two boys were so much alike that their own mother could not tell them apart at times. As young schoolboys, they would often try to confuse their friends and teachers. While they were as mischievous as most boys are, they stayed out of trouble and followed the rules of their father's house. It would not have been safe nor smart for the boys to cross their father, who was a strong, imposing man. His hands were more powerful than tender and his rules far more strict than forgiving.

## Clothed in Different Garments

As the boys grew older, their lives began to take different paths. One of the brothers kept close to his father's rules, stayed out of trouble, and caused no one any harm. The other brother, however, began to bend and then break his father's rules. He soon became seduced by the lure of a wealthy lifestyle and grew ever more distant from his family and home. The fine clothes, fine foods, and fine homes of those "uptown" became too compelling to resist, and soon he was willing to do anything to possess them as well.

Over the next few years the brothers rarely spoke or met. The one twin clothed himself in the garments of compromise and crime, while the other brother clothed himself in the garments of the priesthood. The two who were once identical in attributes and attitudes became polar opposites—one a humble man of the cloth, the other a proud man of the world; one a virtuous man, the other virtueless.

One day the brother who lived to pursue wealth at any cost killed another man in broad daylight and in cold blood. His trial was swift, the evidence against him certain. The judge sentenced him to death in the gas chamber. The life that brother had lived, no matter the cost, would soon cost him his life.

## The Substitute

The day of his execution, a priest came to the prison to see the man condemned to die. Even though the condemned man had no use for piety, he allowed the priest a moment's visit. As the closing cell door secluded the two men, the vertical shafts of light from the prison window illuminated the familiar face of the priest. It was the condemned man's own likeness, the face of his twin brother.

The priest told his brother he had but one purpose for coming today—to set him free.

"Whaddya talkin' about?" the condemned brother asked. He knew that escape was impossible; his appeals were exhausted, and the law demanded his imminent death.

"I will take your place," the priestly brother whispered. "I shall take your clothes, your sentence, and your punishment. You then shall take my clothes, my reputation, and my freedom." He laid out the plan as firmly as he could, evoking memories of their father to forestall his brother's argument. "I would only ask that you do one thing," he added as he exchanged his clothes and his life with his brother.

"Whatzat? I'll do anything. Anything you ask," the soon-to-be-free convict swore as he put on his brother's clerical collar.

"Live worthy of the garments I am giving you," the priest said as he finished putting on the soiled likeness of his condemned brother.

"Do I havta? Ya know I ain't no goody-goody priest," he admitted. "I mean, once I'm free, I'm free, right? No strings?"

"No strings. Only my request." The priestly brother sat down on the solitary stained mattress. "Consider it to be your thanks to me— that is all I ask."

With that, the guard opened the door and motioned for the new-born "priest" to come with him. "Right this way, Father. We're ready to go now."

"Hey, who you call—uh . . . Go where, my son?"

"It's time for this scum to pay for his crimes." The surly guard spoke as he jerked forward the willing arm of the surrogate brother.

As his brother walked toward the gas chamber without hesitation, the novice priest desperately considered all his options. Could he overpower the guards and set them both free? How? And how could he get away impersonating a priest when he had forgotten even how to tell the truth or do one right thing? Why was his brother doing this? What did this mean? As they neared the gas chamber, the priestly collar around his neck grew increasingly uncomfortable.

Without a word the guards secured the doomed man in the gas chamber, the silence broken only by the clinical sounds of the preparation for death. The priest broke into a cold sweat as he watched, increasingly confused and unable to intervene.

Then as one brother's life disappeared in the cloud of toxic smoke, the other was set free. By the sacrifice of one, the other was brought from incarceration to liberation. One life exchanged for another. One ending, another beginning. A life purchased by the innocent one who took upon himself the penalty of the guilty. A life now clothed in unearned garments of goodness.

### The True Hero

Who is the hero of this story? Is it the condemned criminal who accepted the unconditional gift of freedom? Is it the legal system that condemned a guilty man, the guards who brought him to justice, or the executioner who carried out the sentence?

Obviously, it is none of these. The hero of this story is the one who took upon himself the garments of a criminal, paying for the other's crimes with his own life.

What kind of hero is Jesus? He is unlike any other. This is the hero of Romans 8:3-4, the hero of the gospel story. He is the one who did what the Law could not do—set us free.

## WHO ARE YOUR HEROES?

When James Lovell, Fred Haise, and Jack Swigert faced the unthinkable, they needed the help of heroes. The superlative effort of Mission Control and the technicians, scientists, and fellow astronauts was their only hope of survival. The men trapped in their lonely, fragile spacecraft so far from home had a hope because when they called for help, heroes were there to answer.

Who are your heroes?

Whom do you call when your life spins out of control?

Who is on the other end of the line when disaster strikes your life—when things blow up, fall apart, crash down, and begin to sink?

I am convinced that we can have hope when life comes undone because there is a hero who hears us when we call. Jesus Christ is qualified to guide us home. He knows how we are made, and He has been where we are. He is, of all men, most qualified.

> We have this hope as an anchor for the soul, firm and secure. It enters the inner sanctuary behind the curtain, where Jesus, who went before us, has entered on our behalf. He has become a high priest forever, in the order of Melchizedek. . . .
>
> Therefore, since we have a great high priest who has gone through the heavens, Jesus the Son of God, let us hold firmly to the

*faith we profess. For we do not have a high priest who is unable to sympathize with our weaknesses, but we have one who has been tempted in every way, just as we are—yet was without sin. Let us then approach the throne of grace with confidence, so that we may receive mercy and find grace to help us in our time of need.*[4]

God took every opportunity to communicate the heroism of Jesus Christ through His Word. The threads of His character and traces of His sacrifice are woven through every book of the Bible. Paul also reminds us when we are struggling to find hope that Jesus Christ accomplished what even God's powerful Law could not. His surpassing greatness merits our hope.

## ALL THAT WE CANNOT DO, HE DOES

*Nobody gives you something for nothing.*
*There's no such thing as a free lunch.*
*You get what you pay for.*
*You've got to pull your own weight.*
*If you want something done right, do it yourself.*
*Anything worth having is worth working for.*
*Hard work is its own reward.*
*Early to bed, early to rise makes a man healthy, wealthy, and wise.*
*A hard-working man is his own best friend.*
*Never trust a man with soft hands.*
*Be your own man.*
*God helps those who help themselves.*

These are just a few of the familiar proverbs from the Gospel of Self-Reliance taught me by my grandfather and father. I am sure that many of you could add other sayings to this list, especially if you were raised as I was.

Many of my family role models were people—farmers, specifically—who made their living with their hands, not their fingers. These people ingrained in me the value of a self-reliant work ethic at an early age. I learned as a young boy that the corn never planted itself.

I observed that the beans and potatoes never walked to your plate on their own. I found out too quickly that milk didn't come from cartons; it came from stupid, ornery, smelly critters that had to be milked, rain or shine, whether you wanted to or not, early—very early—every day.

Where I came from, you worked hard so that you never needed anybody to give you anything. If you could do it yourself, you were expected to get it done—no excuses. No one else was going to do it for you. I was taught that this world owed you nothing, and if you wanted to make something of yourself, the only one who could do it was you. I was taught that hard work was something to be proud of and that self-reliance was a great virtue.

## LIFE BEYOND REPAIR

Last Tuesday afternoon I sat with a wonderful couple from our church who would not have found this advice very helpful. It was not because they did not want advice; they were begging to know what to do. Nor was it because they did not have problems; they were facing the greatest trial they had ever experienced. And neither was it because they did not want answers; they would have given anything to know the answer to just one question: "Why?"

Yet to tell them that they had the strength or the responsibility to handle this crisis on their own would have been, in my opinion, sin. They were confused and deeply wounded by the tragedy that had exploded within their lives without warning and without cause. Just getting through the next moment, the next hour, the rest of the day seemed impossible. The child whose birth they had been anticipating, whom they had already named and made a part of their lives and family, was suddenly gone. While a theology of self-sufficiency may work for milking cows, it has no place at the death of a loved child.

If we could control every detail of our lives and the lives of those we love, a work-ethic theology would be sufficient. But when things happen that we cannot anticipate, control, or manipulate, then our theology needs some help, and so do we. Self-reliance can take us only so far. It cannot give us hope when we are left helpless. It cannot get us all the way home.

You may know all too well the feeling of having your hands tied as you helplessly watch your life or the lives of others spin out of control. You may have seen times when all of your effort, all of your striving, and all of your hard work could not bring everything back in line. We would like to believe that only good things happen to good people and bad things happen only to bad people. The problem is, if we are honest, we find that this is not true.

### Responsibility: Responding to His Ability

God, through His Son Jesus Christ, provides those who follow Him with the power of His Spirit. The Holy Spirit then enables those who are saved by grace to fulfill the righteous requirements of the Law. We vicariously fulfill the requirements of the Law—in that we are made holy through the sacrifice of Jesus Christ. *The letter* of the Law is fulfilled in us—through Him.

It is also true that we then reflect the righteous requirements of the Law when we live by His Spirit rather than by our sinful flesh. When believers live worthy of their redemption, they are fulfilling *the spirit* of the Law of God. The righteous requirements of the Law were fulfilled in and by Christ, but the essence of the Law, loving God and serving others, is fulfilled in the lives of believers. In this way, by being in Christ we are responding to God's ability, and we fulfill the responsibility of the Law of God.

### Living Worthy of Our Garments

Following the execution of his innocent brother, the born-again priest walked the streets he had once walked as a criminal. Abandoning the garments of the priesthood, he returned to the clubs and bars where he had spent his former life in pursuit of pleasure. He sought out his former friends and associates, but all the while his brother's words replayed in his thoughts: *Live worthy of the garments I am giving you.*

Haunted by his brother's sacrifice, the redeemed man determined that he would change his ways. He decided the only right thing to do was to carry on the work of his brother and to live as his brother would. But he was too weak; the temptations were too great; his old life was too deeply ingrained. He repeatedly tried and failed. But he never gave up. His brother's death had changed something inside him that made it impossible to be comfortable in his former life.

He soon found that the only way to adhere to his new lifestyle was to wear the priestly garments his brother had given him, to openly display his transformed life. When he walked through the streets in his old clothes, he found himself doing the things he used to do. But dressed in his brother's clothes, he was better able to resist his old lifestyle.

The struggle remained, but the constant reminders—the collar around his neck, the people who called him "Reverend" and "Father," and the requests for help and advice—helped him grow increasingly free of his old life. Eventually, even though the conflict never completely died, he began to do the work of his brother. He did it not because he had to, but because he was grateful to be truly free.

## MISSION PROTOCOL

In the final minutes of its mission, Apollo 13 hurtled toward the earth at 24,000 miles an hour. All that the crew had been through over the last four days was just moments from ending. As the tiny command module became enveloped in the flames of reentry, radio contact with Mission Control was lost.

While this was normal for every mission reentry, for Apollo 13 these minutes would seem like hours. Through three agonizing minutes, the people who had been busy every moment of the last four days trying to save the crew of Apollo 13 could do nothing but wait in silence.

When television cameras on board the recovery ship spotted the parachutes of Apollo 13 descending safely into the Pacific Ocean, a spontaneous cheer erupted in Mission Control. The celebration mushroomed into sheer pandemonium as the exhausted team watched Haise, Swigert, and Lovell climb out of their bobbing spacecraft. By the time the helicopters landed on the recovery carrier and the three men walked on deck, Mission Control was in full Mardi Gras. They had done the impossible, and their joy was uncontained.

## SAFE AT HOME

America sent four more teams of Apollo astronauts to the moon after Apollo 13. On each mission the team of scientists, technicians, astronauts, and engineers worked with the mission crew every mile of the way. In the ten Apollo missions that traveled from Earth to the moon, not a single crew member was lost.

There will be a day when we also arrive safely home. I am as certain of this as I am of my own life. I know that our mission is being guided and guarded by one who knows everything there is to know about the design and the details of our mission. He never sleeps; He is always available, with us every step of the way. I know that He has never lost one of His own—each one has made it safely home. And I also know that the protocol requires a celebration to begin the moment a lost and lonely traveler comes home.

This is our hope.

I can't wait.

# THREE

# The Test
# of Hope

*Those who live according to the sinful nature*
*have their minds set on what that nature desires;*
*but those who live in accordance with the Spirit*
*have their minds set on what the Spirit desires.*
*The mind of sinful man is death,*
*but the mind controlled by the Spirit is life and peace;*
*the sinful mind is hostile to God.*
*It does not submit to God's law,*
*nor can it do so.*
*Those controlled by the sinful nature cannot*
*please God.*

*Romans 8:5-8*

It was close to one o'clock in the morning before we finally returned
to our hotel. What began five hours earlier as a brief one-hour trip into
the hills east of Los Angeles had turned into a tour of southern
California's extensive freeway system and a rude lesson in gender-
based navigational techniques.

## LOST ANGELES

By the time we had arrived at the typical suburban home on the outskirts of LA, it was just getting dark. The subdivision was one of those
endlessly repetitious cookie tins of a development, the kind where
every house looks like a different-colored mirror image of the one

down the street and where some genius of a developer named all the streets with such clever names as Rosita, Casita, Conchita, and Repeata.

By ten o'clock that evening we had not yet located the freeway, and the lights of LA were just a distant glow on the horizon. Being neither a resident nor a regular visitor to southern California, I would have been wise to stop and (A) get directions or (B) get a map. However I chose option (C) none of the above. That evening we drove without a map over 150 miles for almost five hours at night on streets I had never seen—but I was *never* lost.

At this point some speculative commentary may be useful to explain the psycho-geographic phenomenon taking place in our rental car just east of Los Angeles that night. This behavior is all too common among men in America—so common in fact that you could even call it epidemic.

I was overcome by a hormone-induced condition that physically and emotionally prohibited me from doing anything rational like asking for directions or buying a map. I call this condition *"hormonally induced gender-based navigational certitude"*—HIGNaC, for all you military types.

My theory of HIGNaC is built upon both biological and environmental factors. Biologically speaking, this cartographic crisis may be directly linked to male DNA.[1] Genetically speaking, this theory states that the chromosomes that distinguish men from women are somehow directional because they are electromagnetically charged. The presence of the Y chromosome in the male body thus creates some kind of electromagnetic polarization that causes a man's chemical balance to respond directionally like a compass. If, as it has been said, women are born with a biological clock, then men are born with a biological compass.

### The Conspiracy

In addition to these biological and genetic factors present in men since the dawn of time, societal and cultural influences compound this problem. These influences accentuate and validate a man's sense of his biological compass, thereby rendering him incapable of ever even thinking he is lost. From the time a boy is taught to run to first base and not to third, he realizes that much of his manhood depends upon knowing, or at least pretending to know, in which direction he is headed.

Therefore, this total anthropological conspiracy leaves us without much hope, for it transcends even the simple hypothetical biological factors alone. It is a grand conspiracy that constrains a man from not only admitting that he gets lost, but from even realizing that he *is* lost.

BEING LOST IS FOR WIMPS. This all-important ideological conviction comes from almost every cultural and historical source. It is inscribed in the ancient traditions of the American movie-going, television-watching male tribal history. It is imprinted on the American male psyche like a tattoo: Heroes never get lost. Period. John Wayne was never lost. Columbus never asked for directions; he just pointed his boat and sailed off into history. Do you think that those astronauts with "The Right Stuff" ever go the wrong way? No way.

Psychologically speaking, being lost requires admitting that you need help to find where you are going. Admitting that you need help is the same as admitting you cannot do it yourself. Admitting you cannot do it yourself is admitting weakness. Admitting weakness is, as we all know, for wimps.

Call it macho, call it ego, call it stupido, call it what you will, there is hardly a man alive who would not rather pretend to know where he is than to have to admit that he does not know his head from a hole in the ground. To admit confusion publicly, especially in front of women and children, is a sign of weakness. Just the thought of it is enough to bring tears to John Wayne's eyes.

NOT KNOWING WHERE YOU ARE GOING MAKES YOU LOOK LIKE AN IDIOT. On Sunday afternoon, October 28, 1964, Minnesota Viking defensive lineman Jim Marshall recovered a fumble in a game against the San Francisco 49ers. This was one of the twenty-nine fumbles Marshall recovered in his eighteen-year Hall-of-Fame career. However, what made this fumble recovery the most memorable of his career is that Marshall rambled with the ball sixty yards into the end zone—*the wrong end zone*. As his teammates chased him, as the fans and coaches screamed, Jim Marshall ran over half the length of the football field into his own end zone.

Even though Marshall was one of the best to ever play his position, he could not help looking something less than Hall-of-Fame material just then. This experience illustrates just how stupid a man can look when his biological compass malfunctions.

YOUR PARENTS TAUGHT YOU NEVER TO TALK TO STRANGERS. We have all at one time or another been asked by some stranger for directions. Most of the time we can tell these innocent tourists how to get where they want to go. However, sometimes we give people directions and then realize after they have driven away that we told them the wrong thing. Even though it was completely unintentional, we sent them right when we meant left, and when we told them to take the third road after the light, we really meant the fourth road before the light.

It also occasionally happens that when someone asks us for directions, we can only approximate where something is, so we simply do our best to aim them right and send them on their way hoping they'll either find it or ask someone who really knows. We're just trying to be polite. Think about it—if you've done it, even unintentionally, to someone else, why wouldn't that person do it to you?

Worse than this, however, are the pathfinder/direction-givers who are also pathological liars. You don't know who they are. In fact you don't even know *where* you are, so you won't know it when they send you to Timbuktu just for laughs. Why should you believe these people? They could be banjo-playing, eyeless psychopaths for all you know.

What if they are not malicious or psychotic, but just so clueless about directions that they don't even know *that they don't know* that what they're telling you is wrong? How do you know you're not asking the village idiot for directions?

Didn't your parents teach you better than this? If you're smart enough not to talk to strangers, what kind of a moron is going to talk to you? Listen to your parents. It's a big, bad world out there, and in most cases, it's just not advisable to ask. This is how real men think.

IF YOU STOPPED EVERY TIME YOU WERE LOST, YOU'D NEVER GET ANYPLACE. This is a simple question of time management. The time you spend reading a map or looking for someone to ask for directions is better spent trying to get back to where you are going. If you should somehow grow desperate enough to decide to stop and ask for directions, you must then find someone who looks like he might know what you are looking for. This takes time. So does buying a map and then unfolding it, reading it, folding it back up, and getting underway again. By the time you have finished finding out where you are, you could have gotten miles closer to where you are supposed to be.

The decision to stop to find out where you are and how to get where you are going should be weighed carefully. It always feels better to be moving and lost than to be stopped and lost. In our go-go society, who has time to be lost? Remember, men know that time is money and stopping takes time—which is to say, it costs too much money to ask for directions. It is just a question of being a good steward of your resources.

NOT BEING LOST HELPS SOCIETY. We live in a better world because men will not admit that they are lost. The inability to cope with being lost leads to improved technology and to a booming economy. Take, for example, Global Positioning Systems (GPS). GPS devices will soon be available in most cars. Using satellite positioning technology, these computerized onboard maps display your current location and a road map with destination instructions. Even today you can get a hand-held GPS that will pinpoint your exact location anywhere on the globe, and you don't even need to be in a car. If everyone stopped to ask for directions, we never would have needed to invent such a neat device. You do your part to contribute to the economy by not asking for directions. It's not only manly; it's downright patriotic.

### The Epidemic of Lostness

These five points are, of course, tongue-in-cheek, and this stubborn macho behavior is only a stereotype, although it closely resembles the truth. Not all men, and not *only* men, are afraid to ask for directions or are too stubborn to consult a map. Yet this behavior is common enough for most of us to identify with at least one such experience as either participants or observers.

The real problem is not in our reluctance to ask for directions but in our reluctance to admit we are lost. Such an admittance requires a humble willingness to trust someone or something other than our own senses and abilities, something most people do not easily do.

## GET LOST

Spiritually speaking, this is a profound truth—it is much easier to get lost than to admit that we are lost. In fact, spiritually, all people are lost from the start, and we are naturally inclined to stay that way. We all enter this life as one would a dark unknown, a hall of mirrors, and have to grope and stumble our way through. Along the way we follow the examples of others, we follow maps drawn up by those who say they know the way, we trust in man-made navigational techniques, and we listen for voices calling us home. Some people strike out on their own; others travel with a group; yet all of us are equally lost right from the start.

In our study of the subject of hope, it is important to realize that on our own, we are hopelessly lost. All this talk of hope is pointless if we do not realize that our hope begins with a recognition of our own hopelessness.

In Jesus Christ, God entered into the marketplace of life. He came to the crowded streets of humanity where we were wandering lost and alone. He found us, He redeemed us, and, as the Holy Spirit, He walks with us through life. He guides us through the maze and through the darkness. The place where our hope begins is where we meet Him—where we stop and ask Him for directions.

In Romans 8:5-8 the apostle Paul looks back to this crossroad of hope. He reminds us what it means to be lost and contrasts this with what it means to be found.

How do you know if you are lost?

How can you know if someone you know is lost?

If the most difficult step in finding hope is admitting that we are lost, these four verses in Romans 8 prompt us to ask some hard questions. They cut right to the chase. Their purpose is to highlight just how lost anyone is apart from Christ.

## ARE YOU CONSISTENTLY UNCONCERNED
## WITH GOD'S DESIRES?

The first question we must face if we are finding it difficult to admit that we are lost concerns our desires. The things we desire are a strong indication of where we really are in life, for what is in our hearts reflects our genuine direction and location in life.

Romans 8:5 is like a spiritual EKG, a sort of scriptural electrocardiogram. The catheter of truth probes into our hearts to see if there are any hindrances or blockages. This test consists of examining our desires by comparing natural with supernatural desires: *"Those who live according to the sinful nature have their minds set on what that nature desires; but those who live in accordance with the Spirit have their minds set on what the Spirit desires."*

### TRUE LOVE

They had been married for almost fifty years when she was diagnosed with Alzheimer's disease. Gradually this once-spirited and godly woman began to lose her strength, her memory, and her dignity. As the disease robbed her of her physical and mental capacities, she became dependent on her loving husband.

Over the next few years he devoted himself to her care, even when she did not know who he was or why he was there. He cared for her every need, every day, right to the end. Never have I witnessed a greater commitment to a relationship. In all my life I think I will never see a more faithful demonstration of love.

An obvious indication of a relationship's strength is each person's concern for the desires of the other. Good parents care about their children's desires. What the boss or the company or the customer wants is of concern to a good employee. In a committed marriage the husband and wife are concerned about each other's needs, and they seek to meet the other's desires.

Conversely, a lack of concern is an indication of a poor relationship. This concern, or lack of it, is also an indication of the condition of our relationship with God. If we are committed to a relationship with Jesus Christ, then we should be concerned about His desires.

## DO YOU MIND?

My grandparents used to tell me to "mind them." It was an instruction pregnant with meaning. To "mind" my grandparents meant more than to simply do what they said; it meant, as they put it, "to pay them mind." This was not just obedience; it was also thoughtfulness, respect, honor, and a compliant attitude. When they reported to my parents that I was not "paying them any mind," I got into serious trouble. Unfortunately, we do not use this phrase much anymore, though we can clearly apply its meaning. We could say that a person who has a good relationship with God "minds God" and that a person who has a poor relationship with God "pays Him no mind."

Do you mind? What is on your mind? What fills your mind? Does God ever cross your mind? That is to say, do you "mind" God? Are you concerned with God's desires? This is the first indication of a true relationship with God or the lack of one.

## ARE YOU CONSTANTLY DISSATISFIED WITH LIFE?

Genuine hope provides us with a unique sense of contentment. Those who have found genuine hope can be content regardless of their situation. If the first indication of our true spiritual location is our desires, the second indication is our satisfaction—or lack of it—with what we have. While none of us should ever be fully satisfied with our existence this side of heaven, constant dissatisfaction is not the mark of someone who knows where he or she is headed.

Do you know contentment?

Or are you consistently dissatisfied in your relationships, possessions, and positions?

Do your desires seem perpetually unfulfilled?

Does the idea of contentment seem foreign, impossible?

### NEO-EPICUREANISM

Aristippus was a philosopher who lived in North Africa over 2,400 years ago. Once a pupil of the great philosopher Socrates, Aristippus is thought to be the founder of the Cyrenaic school of philosophy. This philosophy was refined and eventually overtaken early in the third century B.C. by the more popular philosophy of Epicurus. Even though none of Aristippus's personal writings remain, his motto, "I possess, I am not possessed," and the Cyrenaic slogan, "Eat, drink, and be merry, for tomorrow we die," survived to be integrated into Epicurus's teachings.

The essence of the Epicurean philosophy was an ethic of pleasure. Epicureanism was a sophisticated, materialistic philosophy that identified pleasure as the aim of life, but true pleasure was defined as the absence of pain, the avoidance of trouble, and freedom from annoyance.

Sound familiar? It should. You could say that we live in an age of Neo-Epicureanism. Pleasure is considered by many to be the chief aim in life—as long as it doesn't cause hassles. The mottoes, "I possess, I am not possessed," and "Eat, drink, and be merry, for tomorrow we die," are alive and well among a new generation of Americans.

The pursuit of hassle-free happiness has compelled our Neo-Epicurean society to accumulate wealth and to seek ease of life on an unprecedented scale:

> Consider the fact that the average person living in America today is four times richer than were his or her grandparents who lived at the turn of the twentieth century—and yet we're convinced that we're losing our economic edge and capacity. Even compared to adults in 1950, the typical American today owns twice as many cars, drives nearly three times as far, consumes more than twenty times the volume of plastic, is more than five times as likely to have a home fitted with central air conditioning. We live in a home complete with many devices that did not even exist forty years ago but which have become "indispensable" today, including microwave ovens, video cassette recorders, cordless telephones, and color television sets. We pursue these riches, regardless of the environmental, interpersonal, or emotional consequences of such usage, because we believe they have the power to fulfill our lives.[2]

However, the statistics also show us that while we are living more hassle-free lives, we are not free from stress, and while we are stock-

piling possessions more rapidly than ever before, we are no more satisfied with our lives. Over the last forty years the percentage of
Americans who identify themselves as "very happy" has remained the
same or decreased slightly in spite of our exponentially increased
wealth.[3] As it turns out, our Neo-Epicureanism has proven to be an
ultimately unsatisfying way of life. But this is anything but new news.

### The Mind of Death

The home of Epicurean philosophy in Paul's day was the city of
Corinth. In Paul's first letter to the church in Corinth, he references
the futility of the Epicurean motto: "If the dead are not raised, '*Let us
eat and drink, for tomorrow we die.*'"

As we consider the message of Romans 8:6, the subtle emptiness
and futility of an Epicurean lifestyle is still apparent in his words: "*The
mind of sinful man is death, but the mind controlled by the Spirit is life
and peace.*"

When Paul says that "the mind of sinful man is death," he does
not mean that this person thinks of nothing but death all the time.
This is not meant to depict some Stephen King horror freak who
thinks nothing but ghoulish and macabre thoughts. Rather, the
description speaks of someone whose natural mind is empty of true
meaning—dead—whose values, priorities, and philosophy add up to
little more than a hollow Epicurean way of life. If the only things that
really matter to someone are the things of this life, if he believes this
is all there is, then his is not a life-mind; it is a death-mind. This mind
is ultimately without any real hope.

### He Who Dies with the Most Toys Wins

Nothing exemplifies this mind-set of death more clearly than the now-
familiar bumper sticker I have seen on more than one exclusive sports
car: "Whoever dies with the most toys wins." In other words, all that
matters in life is acquiring a lot of stuff—just in time to die. To pursue
a life in which acquiring all of the finer things in life with a minimal
amount of hassle and stress just in time to die—this is Neo-
Epicureanism at its finest.

As we discussed earlier, the youngest generation of Americans is in many cases reacting with appropriate despair to this hassle-free, pleasure-ethic philosophy. Their apathy can be summed up in one word: *whatever*.

In this honest expression this generation swimming in the wake of their parents' unbridled materialism clearly exhibits the lack of peace found in "Epicureanism." In some sense it is a rejection of what Paul calls the "natural mind-set." Among these "Baby Busters" the pointlessness of even selfishness is producing an attitude that absolutely nothing matters, not even death.

> It's easy to feel confused these days. On the one hand, things seem better than ever. There have been groundbreaking advances in medicine, science, agriculture, international relations, education, and even leisure. On the other hand when you go to bed at night, you may be stumped by two simple questions: "So what was the purpose of today's toils? And why should I get out of bed tomorrow?"
>
> *Such questions are not raised when life is undeniably satisfying.*[4]

Unfortunately many of the people who have discovered the dissatisfaction of this philosophy of life have yet to discover the genuine alternative.

## ROLLING STONES THEOLOGY

Are you constantly dissatisfied with your life?

Do you struggle each day to find contentment, meaning, and purpose?

Is the pursuit of happiness only a pursuit, never a reality?

Does the accumulation of wealth, power, and status leave a hollow feeling in your heart?

To loosely quote that badly dressed Neo-Epicurean theologian Mick Jagger, have you got any "satisfaction" lately?

Romans 8:6 speaks of the mind of the Spirit as the only real alternative to the natural mind. The Spirit is the only one who can produce life and peace. In contrast to the mind of death, the mind of the Spirit results in a sense of satisfaction and confidence in life. The mind of the Spirit is a mind focused on God's activities and God's commands. Pleasing God gives our lives a purpose that can produce lasting satisfaction and contentment. This genuine satisfaction is only a product of the Holy Spirit at work in our lives.

## CORNERSTONE THEOLOGY

If this contentment does not come from our circumstances and our "stuff," then where does it come from?

What is the secret to satisfaction for those who have the mind of the Spirit?

I believe that the cornerstone of contentment is purpose in life. Knowing that everything has a purpose, a confident assurance that there is plan in which we play an important part, builds this cornerstone for our lives.

In Ephesians 2:10, Paul reminds us that our lives do have significance and purpose. This is the design of God: *"For we are God's workmanship, created in Christ Jesus to do good works, which God prepared in advance for us to do."*

When we have a mind-set controlled by the Spirit of God, we find satisfaction in accomplishing those things "which God prepared in advance for us to do." We can find contentment because we know there is purpose and meaning in the circumstances of our lives.

The mind of the Spirit is focused on the purpose of God and on the thoughts that lead to life and peace, just as the mind of the flesh is focused on the pointlessness of life without God and on the thoughts that inevitably lead to death.

Consider Paul's advice in Philippians 4:6-8:

> Do not be anxious about anything, but in everything, by prayer and petition, with thanksgiving, present your requests to God. And the peace of God, which transcends all understanding, will guard your hearts and your minds in Christ Jesus.
>
> Finally, brothers, whatever is true, whatever is noble, whatever is right, whatever is pure, whatever is lovely, whatever is admirable—if anything is excellent or praiseworthy—think about such things.

Romans 8:6 tells us that the mind controlled by the Spirit leads to life and peace. The road map to this perspective is written on the hearts and minds of those who think on the things of God. The promise is that those who are of a spiritual mind-set will know life and peace. Their satisfaction, motivation, and passion will be to please God and to follow His desires. Their contentment comes when they recognize that their lives can make a difference that matters to God and is pleasing to Him. Without this motivation, satisfaction is fleeting, and contentment in life is strictly a matter of keeping score.

### ARE YOU COMPLETELY UNAFFECTED BY GOD'S WORD?

The third question posed by Romans 8:5-8 is perhaps the most straightforward of the difficult questions we are considering in this chapter:

Do you even care?

Does God's instruction matter to you?

Is it possible for you to know what God says and to turn away unconcerned?

If God's Word does not have any real impact on your life, if you can look at the map and still go your own way without regard for where God wants you to go, then most likely you are lost. It is not a problem of difficulty; it is a problem of disobedience.

Do you know someone whose concern for right and wrong is arbitrary and circumstantial?

Are there people in your life who seem concerned with what the Bible says one minute and then go do exactly the opposite the next?

Romans 8:7-8 contains one of the most confrontational statements in the entire Bible as Paul points a finger and asks, Do you even have the capacity to care?

#### THE PORTRAIT OF DESPAIR

The twentieth-century artist Francis Bacon has captured on canvas some of the most disturbing images ever painted. Unlike other modern artists who use graphic or even pornographic images to shock the viewer, Bacon haunts the imagination without blatant vulgarity.

His painting *Study After Velázquez: Portrait of Pope Innocent X* is a smeared and distorted rendering of Velázquez's famous portrait of Pope Innocent X. In this work, Bacon places the muted image of Innocent X in a thinly defined cube laid within a fury of broad vertical streaks. The top of the portrait dissolves into this violent streaking motion, creating a central focus on the gaping mouth of a man, surrounded by a thin cube, seemingly cascading into oblivion. As much as any image ever placed on canvas, Bacon's portrait captures the feeling of complete despair, alienation, and hopelessness. Bacon's images, portraying people trapped in their own futility, capture this sense of hopelessness. These are the visual images of just what it means to be lost.

### The Image of a Lost Man

The apostle Paul paints with words what Francis Bacon created with oils on canvas. Romans 8:7-8 is perhaps one of the most hopeless images in the entire Bible. While the final words of these verses are theologically controversial, they are not ambiguous, being about as subtle as Bacon's portraits. For it is here that Paul makes plain the hopelessness of a lost person's condition.

These two verses indicate that those who are hostile to God not only do not obey Him, but they *cannot* obey Him, nor do they have the capacity to please Him. They do not have the ability in and of themselves to even recognize their need, much less to find their way out of their lost condition. They are not just lost; they are unable even to realize that they are lost. It has been said, they are hopelessly helpless, for, "No man can free himself from himself."

This is intended to be as hopeless as it sounds. This verbal image is meant to be as shocking as a Francis Bacon portrait in its depiction of total despair. To be lost is a desperate condition. To be separated from God is to be truly lost, for in this separation there is total blindness. To be spiritually lost is to be lost without even the capacity to realize that you are lost. For according to these verses, we cannot find our way to heaven; we have to be rescued and taken there. A lost person cannot find what he does not know exists.

### Difficult or Disobedient?

My wife, Diane, is a master teacher. She is not only vastly experienced in working with young children, but she also has a God-given gift in this area. According to her, there is an important difference between a child whose behavior is difficult and a child whose behavior is disobedient. While difficult behavior can have a variety of causes, truly disobedient behavior is the product of one primary cause—a willful disregard for instruction.

Romans 8:7-8 begins by going straight to the point: ". . . *the sinful mind is hostile to God. It does not submit to God's law, nor can it do so."* While we all struggle to live according to God's instruction, this verse is describing more than simple difficulty or an occasional act of disobedience. Romans 8:7 describes a continuous disregard for God's instruction. This disregard acts without regrets and without concern. It is a willful antagonism toward God. This is different from simply not doing the right thing; this is knowing the right thing to do and yet deliberately doing the wrong thing. The light is red; you see it, and you choose to ignore it.

The word translated as "hostile" used to be translated as "enmity"—a word we do not often use in conversation anymore. Most dictionaries define *enmity* as "the feelings that enemies have for each other," and they offer *hostility* and *animosity* as synonyms. This conveys the idea of someone who has more than an occasional difficulty with God's instructions. It is someone who flat-out ignores Him and deliberately disobeys Him.

We all have difficulty in our obedience. There are times when I know what God wants me to do, and I do not do it. In fact, sanctification, which is never complete in this life, is the process of increasing our consistency and conformity to God's desires. You could say that being truly lost is not an occasional wrong turn or missed exit but a complete disregard of all of God's road signs.

The "sinful mind" of Romans 8:7 does not and cannot submit to God's Word. This is similar to a man lost on an uncharted island who does not know how to be rescued and does not even desire to be. No matter how obvious the truth may seem to us or how blatant the reality, the sinful mind can no more submit to God's Word than a person will agree to be rescued if he doesn't think he is lost. Those who cannot submit to God's law do not have the desire nor the capacity to find their way home.

## THE VOICE FROM THE PAST

Romans 8:8 sums up the tragic reality of being lost: *"Those controlled by the sinful nature cannot please God."* Yet this tragedy was not a Pauline creation, for he reflects the truths he learned as a young rabbi studying the words spoken by the prophet Isaiah: *"All of us have become like one who is unclean, and all our righteous acts are like filthy rags; we all shrivel up like a leaf, and like the wind our sins sweep us away."*[5]

These harsh realities also recall the words of Psalms 14:1-3 and 55:1-3, which Paul quoted in Romans 3:9-12:

> *What shall we conclude then? Are we any better? Not at all! We have already made the charge that Jews and Gentiles alike are all under sin. As it is written:*
>
> > *There is no one righteous, not even one;*
> > *there is no one who understands,*
> > *no one who seeks God.*
> > *All have turned away,*
> > *they have together become worthless;*
> > *there is no one who does good,*
> > *not even one.*

Romans 8:5-8 leaves little room for doubt: We are born lost. This condition is made all the more desperate in that we are also born with no sense of direction.

Even when we think we are heading toward God, without His guidance we don't have a clue. Whether we are men or women, young or old, experienced drivers or novice travelers, we are born without the inclination or the capacity to ask for directions. It is not simply a case of hormone-induced navigational certitude; it is a sin-induced blindness to God. The only way we can find our way home is with His guidance, for without it, we are flying blind.

## GPS

A short while ago, I was flying back to Dallas from Alabama with my best friend in his small private plane. Somewhere over the Louisiana-Arkansas border, as the sun began to set, we noticed that the weather was starting to deteriorate. Not only was it getting darker, but the clouds were quickly wrapping around us, and the visibility was decreasing rapidly.

The FAA regional control center in Memphis, which was directing our flight at the time, confirmed that the weather directly ahead of us was getting rough. The controller informed us that severe thunderstorms were building, that we would be hard-pressed to go around them or over them, and it would be best not to try to go through them.

We needed a place to land, and we needed it soon, since our small aircraft would not do well in the turbulence of a severe thunderstorm. When my pilot friend used the words *Cuisinart* and *us* in the same sentence, I knew how serious it was. It took us a few minutes, but we were finally able to admit that we needed to change our flight plan, *right now*.

It was not long before we were completely shrouded in the clouds of the oncoming storm. At that moment our natural senses became useless to us. We were totally dependent upon the voice of the controller, the map in my hands, and the Global Positioning System in the instrument console of the plane. We now had two choices: Follow the instruments precisely or die.

As we searched for available airstrips, another aircraft broke through to the Memphis center on our frequency. It was a much smaller plane without a GPS, radar, or the other IFR capabilities we had. It was also flying right on the leading edge of the line of thunderstorms, and its pilot was unable to see anything. He was starting to get tossed around quite a bit. Yet he was determined to keep going the direction he was headed. Even as the controller advised him repeatedly to revise his flight plan, the pilot kept insisting he could make his own way.

I distinctly remember the tone of this anonymous pilot's voice as he repeatedly asked Memphis Control to direct him around the dangerous weather and on to his destination. Yet even as the regional controller advised him to get out of the weather and down on the ground, the pilot resisted.

The horrifying truth is that we are born flying with less instrumentation and in worse weather than the pilot on that stormy night over Arkansas. We are being tossed about in the violent storms of life, and without Christ, we have no charts, no instruments, no GPS—no real guidance. Many people, ignoring the voice of the Spirit and the Word of God, continue to fly on. Unfortunately they never do get home.

We are desperately lost. We are alone in the storms of life, and by the time we realize the danger, it is often too late. If in our arrogance we try to find our way home alone, or if we ignore the voice of the one who knows the only safe way home, the storms will ultimately destroy us. Even our natural instruments cannot be trusted, for they are incorrectly calibrated. Romans 8:7-8 portrays this desperate isolation in the harshest of terms because this is the most desperate of truths.

As our plane broke through the cloud ceiling above the lighted airstrip, I was thankful that my friend is an excellent and cautious pilot, but I was also thankful that we had the guidance from the map, the controller, and the instruments. We took the controller's advice, and we made the right choice, for just minutes after we put down, a vicious thunderstorm unleashed its ferocity all around us.

We cannot find our way through the storms without help. The message of Romans 8:7-8 makes this clear. It is only by God's grace that we can even recognize our lostness.

Do you or does someone you know live without regard for God's instruction?

Is the Word of God an optional "instrument" in your life?

Have you ever been willing to admit that you are lost and that you need guidance?

Do God's desires as revealed in His Word matter to you?

The storms are out there. You are alone.

Do you know how to get home?

## LOST IN LA—AGAIN

As I work on this chapter, I am back in Los Angeles, where once again I managed to get lost. I think it is best for me to start calling this city *Lost* Angeles. On my way in from the airport, I thought I would take a "shortcut"—which, of course, turned out to be anything but short. Even though my wife was not with me, the old HIGNaC took over. I couldn't help it. I had no control.

I was convinced, as I usually am, that right around the next corner I would find a familiar street. I was convinced of this for over an hour. I was convinced of this as the sun began to set and those young *vatos* sitting next to me at stoplights began to look more and more puzzled by my gringo presence in their community.

But I just kept driving, even with a map right there in the car. When I eventually did stop to look at it, I was still convinced I could find my way back without it. Not until I took the time to look at the map closely did I discover that I was completely on the wrong side of the city, miles from where I was supposed to be. Finally, with the help of the map, I found my way "home."

It took me about four blocks to get lost. In fact I was going the wrong way after my first turn, and yet it took me over an hour to admit that I was lost. Getting lost is easy. Admitting we are lost is hard. But until we have a willingness to admit that we are lost, we will never find our way home.

If you are lost today, or if you know someone who is, there is hope. Even in the most desperate of circumstances, there is hope. In the face of the storms of life, there is hope. There is hope for anyone and everyone who is willing to admit that he or she is lost.

In order to find our hope, we must first find ourselves hopeless.

There is a way home.

# The Spirit
# of Hope

*You, however,*
  *are controlled not by the sinful nature*
  *but by the Spirit,*
  *if the Spirit of God lives in you.*
*And if anyone does not have the Spirit of Christ,*
  *he does not belong to Christ.*
*But if Christ is in you,*
  *your body is dead because of sin,*
  *yet your spirit is alive because of righteousness.*
*And if the Spirit of him*
  *who raised Jesus from the dead*
  *is living in you,*
  *he who raised Christ from the dead*
  *will also give life*
  *to your mortal bodies*
  *through his Spirit,*
  *who lives in you.*

*Romans 8:9-11*

On Wednesday afternoon, April 22, 1992, doctors informed Daniel and Patty Wallace that their eight-year-old son had contracted a very rare and lethal form of renal cell cancer. This carcinoma was so rare that his was the first case diagnosed in a child in the entire United States in eight years.

For the Wallace family the next six months were filled with a series of grueling bone marrow tests and radical chemotherapy. Unless you have been there, you cannot comprehend the devastation that takes place as parents watch their child suffer from such a lethal disease.

Dr. Daniel Wallace is obscenely brilliant. He is able to comprehend things that make my head hurt just thinking about them. His idea of a stimulating afternoon would be to lock himself in his study and read a few ancient manuscripts—in their original languages. He is so smart that I have heard him on more than one occasion quote technical scholarly writings to the letter and cite obscure passages from memory, including where on the page you might find the quotation.

He is an expert in the language, text, and grammar of the Greek New Testament, as well as a popular seminary professor. He is recognized as an expert in his field, and even though he is still relatively young, he holds his own among much longer-tenured scholars. I am also pleased to say that I know him to be a godly man, a committed husband, and a dedicated father. However, early in 1992 when his son was diagnosed with cancer, not only was Dan's son struggling to survive, but so too was the faith of this brilliant scholar.

Miraculously, the boy survived, and so did my friend's faith. Three years later, after reflecting on his experience, Dr. Wallace wrote a thoughtful article about what he had learned for *Christianity Today* titled, "Who's Afraid of the Holy Spirit?"

> I am a cessasionist. That is to say, I believe that certain gifts of the Holy Spirit—namely, the "sign gifts" of healing, tongues, and miracles—were employed in the early church to authenticate that God was doing something new, but that they ceased with the death of the last apostle. This is what distinguishes me from a charismatic Christian, who believes the Holy Spirit still uses sign gifts today.
>
> While I still consider myself a cessasionist, the last few years have shown me that my spiritual life has gotten off track—that somehow I, along with many others in my theological tradition, have learned to do without the third person of the Trinity.[1]

Who is the Holy Spirit?

Do you know who the third person of the Trinity is or what role He plays in your life?

If you do, is your understanding of the Holy Spirit out of balance?

Is it exclusively based either on your experience on the one hand or on sterile biblical data on the other?

Are you confused by the debate and frustrated by the divisiveness this issue stirs up among Christians?

Have you too learned to do without the third person of the Trinity?

## THE AGENT OF HOPE

In our study of Romans 8 and the subject of hope, we dare not avoid the role of the Holy Spirit. He is the person of hope. If God the Father is the *architect* of hope, and Jesus is the *author* of hope, then the Holy Spirit is the *agent* of hope. It is the Holy Spirit who applies the will of God and the work of Christ to our lives. He energizes and empowers hope. Without the Holy Spirit, hope is no help; it is only a theory. According to Gordon Fee: "The Spirit is therefore the key in our new relationship with God, as children who are heirs with Christ of eternal glory. Not only so, but the Spirit is also the key to our enduring present suffering while we await that final glory."[2]

It is important not to be too clinical as we consider what the Spirit does in our lives. We can, like my seminary professor friend, find ourselves so deep in a cognitive faith that we eliminate the emotional and mysterious elements of our walk with Christ and, in so doing, emasculate the work of the Spirit. We can become so academic and logical in our approach that the Comforter who lives in our hearts bears no real witness in our lives. And consequently when we long most for hope, we may *know* hope and yet never *feel* it. It is the work of the Holy Spirit that brings our hope to life.

## THE HOLY SPIRIT
### INDWELLS US

*"You, however, are controlled not by the sinful nature but by the Spirit, if the Spirit of God lives in you. And if anyone does not have the Spirit of*

*Christ, he does not belong to Christ"* (Romans 8:9). The first way that the Spirit of God empowers our hope is by living within us. Theologically speaking, this verse tells us two truths about the indwelling of the Holy Spirit: First, *the presence of the Spirit controls us*, and second, *the absence of the Spirit condemns us*.

These are the facts. The question is not what this verse says, but what it means by what it says. To understand what it means to have the Spirit of God dwelling within us is not simply an academic exercise. Our hope only comes alive when we know by our experience as well as by our exegesis that He lives in us.

## HIS PRESENCE CONTROLS US

The first part of Romans 8:9 literally says, *"But you are not in flesh, but in Spirit, seeing that the Spirit of God has taken up residence in you."* That is to say, He is in your house. The word meaning "dwells" or "to take up residence" is from the Greek word meaning "house." It specifically means to have "a settled permanent penetrative influence." The Holy Spirit is a permanent house guest in the household of your life.

### Holy Spirit Etiquette

People behave in some peculiar ways when they find out that I am a "man of the cloth." I have heard frustrated garage mechanics speak entire sentences without one single expletive. I have watched groups of teenagers make cigarettes and beer cans disappear with the magical skill of David Copperfield. But among all this odd behavior, the most consistently amazing activity I encounter is the response of housewives to a pastoral visit.

It seems to me that I have never been in a dirty home when I was expected. Even homes with a small resident army of preschool ankle-biters, who are bent on destroying everything of value below their eye level, are amazingly spotless when I am invited in.

I have seen working moms who got home ten minutes before I come to their door fix a meal, feed their family, change their clothes, pick up untold amounts of clothes and clutter, and prepare a dessert before I arrive without leaving a dirty dish in sight. I have heard the fathers yelling at their children, "Pick up your junk right now; the preacher's coming over!" even as I rang the doorbell.

Pets are banished, children are hidden, dirty clothes are stuffed in closets, and all manner of stuff is tucked out of sight in order to make a good impression on this pious guest. Believe me, it is hard not to laugh when a sweating, out-of-breath woman welcomes me into her home as the last piece of dirty laundry is being dragged around the corner by a screaming child.

### Guest or Pest?

The Holy Spirit, however, is not just a pious pastoral visitor; He is a permanent resident. He doesn't make visits; He moves in. When He comes, He comes to stay. He is a combination mother-in-law, rich uncle, best friend, nosy neighbor, fire inspector, father, pastor-come-to-live-with-you. His presence in the "household" of your life should have a dramatic effect on the way you live.

Have you ever had long-term house guests? No matter how close you are or how comfortable you feel around them, don't you do things just a little differently?

How differently would you behave if your rich uncle came to stay?

Or what if it were some famous movie star or sports hero?

Or Billy Graham?

Or the President of the United States?

Now imagine that Jesus Christ is moving in. All that you know about His desires, convictions, insights, and power is living with you in your home, in the household of your heart. His presence should control you just as the presence of a house guest controls you.

Perhaps this is where the passion goes away. We get too comfortable, too used to having Him around. We don't go out of our way anymore. We don't watch our language or our attitudes. His residency leads to complacency. We leave our homes in a mess; we don't clean up because we are used to His being around. We don't use the linen napkins—paper will do just fine. The Holy Spirit is no longer someone who affects our behavior because we are unconcerned with doing our best for Him. As they say, "Familiarity breeds contempt." While He is not really a pest, He is no longer a special guest.

## GOD'S TRADEMARK

The second half of verse 9 is a terse warning: *"And if anyone does not have the Spirit of Christ, he does not belong to Christ."* The Holy Spirit dwells in all who place their faith in Jesus Christ. He is the trademark of the work of God. Without it you are a counterfeit, a fraud, a phony. The effect of the Holy Spirit on your life is evidence that He is in your life. As we said in the previous chapter, without that evidence, you have reason to wonder if He is living in you. It is one thing to grow contemptuous because of familiarity; it is another thing entirely to live with no concern whatsoever for the Spirit's work in your life. If the light is not on and there is no fire burning, it may be because there is no one home.

## THE HOLY SPIRIT
## TRANSFORMS US

Can you remember the first time you fell in love? It's said that you never forget your first love. I believe that you never forget the feelings of first love either. The experience of a first love is a compelling life-or-death proposition. A first love is an odd combination of pain and wonder, of excitement and terror, of curiosity and timidity. They don't call them "crushes" for nothing.

This is what it means to be transformed—to be motivated, stimulated, and completely preoccupied with another person. Feeling this way radically changes your behavior. Emotions ebb and flow with the tides of "hello" and "good-bye."

If he says, "Hey, nice outfit. You look great," you will go out and buy a dozen more like it.

If he says, "Gee, those clothes make you look just like your mom," you wouldn't be able to rip off the outfit fast enough to go burn them.

If she says, "I'll see you tonight," nothing that happens between now and then matters. The time cannot pass fast enough. The anticipation of that moment is compelling enough to make a thirteen-year-old boy take a shower in the middle of the week *and* put on aftershave.

If she says, "I can't make it tonight," your day is ruined. Your whole life is not worth living. When you're in love, being with that other person is all that matters. It compels you; it controls you; it changes you.

## CHRIST IN US

Romans 8:10 speaks of a radical transformation, one even more radical than a first love. It is a true life-and-death transformation accomplished by the work of true love through the presence of the Holy Spirit: *"But if Christ is in you, your body is dead because of sin, yet your spirit is alive because of righteousness."*

Regardless of how you understand the idiosyncrasies of this verse, we do know one important fact: If Christ is *in* us, it transforms our life. This transformation happens *to* us, not *because* of us. The death this verse speaks about, whether it means physical death or a "spiritual" death, is a result of the Fall.

Once again we must not simply understand this verse exegetically; we need to know what it means experientially. The truth of this verse must sink down from our heads, past our tight little collars, and into our hearts. The Holy Spirit has rescued us, resuscitated us, and revived us. We once were dead, but He has brought us back to life, and He empowers us to live a transformed life hereafter. We owe Him everything. We owe it to Him to forsake our old ways and live a transformed life.

## THE HOLY SPIRIT
## SECURES US

When I was a freshman in high school in the suburbs of northern New Jersey (all northern New Jersey is a suburb of something), I learned quickly one of the important codes in the land of linoleum and lockers: Freshmen were not welcome in the school bathrooms.

This doubly applied to those freshmen like myself who were somewhat less than—how shall I say it?—physical specimens. Just short of five and a half feet tall and weighing in at less than 100 pounds (with change in my pockets), I certainly could not have been considered intimidating to anyone other than a poor, starving third world refugee.

## BOB SQUARED

At the same time I was learning the laws of the blackboard jungle (and developing extraordinary bladder capacity), I met two freshmen who changed my life. They were both named Bob—at least that is what their tattoos said. I was in the same grade, but I was most definitely not in their class. These guys were from the other end of the gene pool.

Bob and Bob always wore black leather jackets, white T-shirts, and blue jeans. You could hear them coming when they walked because the chains they wore on their jackets, which they had probably pulled off a large tow truck, sounded like the spurs on a gunfighter's boots. They both had hair like Elvis's. Possibly they both had been shaving since kindergarten, which would have been about the time they got their first Harleys. They never took notes, never paid attention, always slept in class, came and left without permission, and parked their motorcycles on the sidewalk, but nobody ever seemed to care. But the strangest thing of all about Bob and Bob was that for some reason known only to God, they liked me.

Because of my association with Bob and Bob, I could do things in that school that no one who looked like me would have dreamed possible. I had power, abilities, and a freedom as I walked down those hallways that had nothing to do with my own skills but everything to do with my friends' reputations. With Bob² on my side, I was an intimidating physical specimen at ninety-eight pounds.

## THE TRANSFORMING PRESENCE

If my life was changed because of two Brylcreem-haired, motorcycle-riding, chain-wearing, leather-clad bullies who hung around with me, how radically should my life be affected when the God of all creation, the maker of heaven and earth, the powerful God almighty loves me and dwells within me? If I grew bold and confident when Bob and Bob stood beside me, how should my confidence grow when the Spirit of the living God dwells within me? That same power, talent, skill, and ability that I gained from my two friends is a dim reflection of what I gain from the Holy Spirit.

## BEEN THERE, DONE THAT

Romans 8:11 is a vivid reminder of the powerful Spirit living within us: *"And if the Spirit of him who raised Jesus from the dead is living in you, he who raised Christ from the dead will also give life to your mortal bodies through his Spirit, who lives in you."*

The formula for energizing our hope is quite simple: If the Spirit who brought Jesus Christ back from the dead lives in us, that same Spirit can bring us back from the dead. As it is said, "Been there. Done that."

### The First Dimension of Security

There are two dimensions to this truth. The first is eschatological—that is to say, yet future. This is the promise of the resurrection. If Jesus was raised by the Spirit, and that exact same Spirit lives in us, then that exact same Spirit will also one day raise us. We have a hope of a future resurrection because of one that happened in the past, and the team that pulled off the first one is the same team that will pull off the future one. Count on it. This is what we are hoping for, and it is not an unfounded hope.

Bob and Bob never had to beat up anyone on my behalf, though they were eager to do it. They never had to intervene to protect me like everyone knew they could. I survived simply on their reputations. At some point in the past, they had caused serious bodily harm to another person, and this was enough. So we anticipate a future resurrection by the power of the Spirit because we know that He has done it before. Our hope is based on His reputation.

### Security's Second Dimension

The second dimension of the truth of verse 11 has a more immediate impact: Our lives here and now are changed by the Spirit of the resurrection. Just as my life was changed by Bob and Bob's presence in my life, so our lives are changed by the presence of the Spirit. The primary way our lives are changed relates directly to our hope: We are made secure.

We are secure in knowing that the Spirit who lives within us keeps His promises. We are secure because there is nothing, not even death, that He cannot conquer. We are secure because we are worth dying for and living with.

When Jesus told His disciples that He would send His "Comforter," He was telling them not only the identity of the Spirit of God, but He was also describing the work of the Holy Spirit. We have comfort because of our Comforter.

This is not meant to be a hollow truth but something we know and feel. It is not simply a case of being secure; it is also a case of feeling secure. Just as a child would cling to a crib blanket for security when far from home, so too the Holy Spirit, the Comforter, provides us with a sense of security when we are far from our "home."

### Quickening

The Holy Spirit provides both a feeling of security and the reality of security. Romans 8:11 tells us that the Holy Spirit gives life to, or "quickens," our mortal bodies.[3] Once again the old English text highlights the activity of the Spirit. The idea of quickening, while uncommon in today's English, gives a more visual sense to the work of the Spirit. "Quicken" does not mean that we can run faster or jump higher; rather, it implies the correct sense that life in the Spirit is more vibrant and full. We can have increased confidence, comfort, and security because of the presence of the Spirit in our lives.

Jesus described it in John 10:10: *"I have come that they may have life, and have it to the full."* More than simple living and breathing, abundant life has purpose and meaning. The Holy Spirit secures our life here and forever.

To know hope without the Holy Spirit is no hope. My point is more than an intellectual and theological issue; it is an issue of theoretical truth versus reality. The Holy Spirit is real, and He is really indwelling us, transforming us, and securing us. These are not simply theological phrases; they are living realities that must be lived realities.

### KNOW HOPE OR NO HOPE

My friend Professor Dan Wallace learned the significance of the living reality of the Holy Spirit as he faced real life, a real hard life.

Mine had become a cognitive faith—a Christianity from the neck up. As long as I could control the text, I was happy. I lived in the half-reality that theological articulation is valid only if it is based on sound exegesis and nothing else.

Through this experience I found that the Bible was not adequate. I needed God in a personal way—not as an object of my study, but as a friend, guide, comforter. I needed an existential experience of the Holy One. Quite frankly, I found that the Bible was not the answer. I found the Scriptures to be helpful—even authoritatively helpful—as a guide. But without my feeling God, the Bible gave me little solace.

As shocking as this may sound to many in the cessasionist circle, the Bible is not a third member of the Trinity.

Eventually we no longer relate to him. God becomes the object of our investigation rather than the Lord to whom we are subject. The vitality of our religion gets sucked out. As God gets dissected, our stance changes from "I trust in . . ." to "I believe that . . ."

Should we not have a reckless abandon in our devotion to him? Should we not throw ourselves on him, knowing that apart from him we can do nothing?[4]

Our relationship with the Holy Spirit is more than a cognitive and intellectual truth that we allow to gather dust on the shelves of our life. The Holy Spirit is a person. He is the person of hope. Our hope is only as real as the presence of the Holy Spirit in our lives.

Not to know Him is to know no hope.

To know Him is to know hope.

# OUR HOPE
# EMPOWERS MINISTRY

# The Economics of Hope

> *Therefore, brothers,*
> *we have an obligation—*
> *but it is not to the sinful nature,*
> *to live according to it.*
> *For if you live according to the sinful nature,*
> *you will die;*
> *but if by the Spirit*
> *you put to death*
> *the misdeeds of the body,*
> *you will live.*
>
> *Romans 8:12-13*

On an average *day* in America:

39,109 pounds of marijuana,
2,239 pounds of cocaine,
23 pounds of heroin
are brought into the United States;

56,061 Americans drive a car after consuming alcohol,
71 die in alcohol-related automobile accidents;

81 Americans commit suicide;

1,849 children are abused,
14 children die from abuse,

4,707 children are reported missing,
1,932 children are abducted, 14 by strangers;
2,740 children run away from home,
514 runaways become involved in illegal activities,
296 become involved in prostitution;

93,474 crimes are committed,
34,474 Americans are arrested,
957 Americans are arrested on charges of fraud,
35 Americans are arrested on charges of embezzlement;

3,786 Americans are assaulted,
1,704 Americans are robbed,
126 Americans are raped,
49 Americans are murdered;

2,433 automobiles are stolen;

41,096 calls are made to dial-a-porn numbers;
1,994 babies are born to unwed mothers; and
3,477 abortions are performed.[1]

## SIN IS SERIOUS BUSINESS

Sin is serious business. In fact, sin is big business, a serious multibillion-dollar big business. It may be impossible to calculate exactly how much money is spent each year in America on sin, as the General Accounting Office produces no such figures. But if it did, the numbers would undoubtedly be enormous. Sin is serious business, because sin is serious.

### Get Serious

In a house in the small Galilean town of Capernaum, Jesus rehearsed a radical lesson with His disciples on the economics of sin. His was not a lesson in international supply-side economics but a lesson about the high cost of sin.

> *If your hand causes you to sin, cut it off. It is better for you to enter life maimed than with two hands to go into hell, where the fire never goes out.*

*And if your foot causes you to sin, cut it off. It is better for you to enter life crippled than to have two feet and be thrown into hell. And if your eye causes you to sin, pluck it out. It is better for you to enter the kingdom of God with one eye than to have two eyes and be thrown into hell.*[2]

In this instruction about the economics of sin, Jesus was not encouraging mutilation as a measure of dedication. He was not advocating amputation as a means of holiness. He was, in the most graphic terms possible, illustrating the seriousness of sin. Sin is serious business, so serious that radical choices must be made in order to avoid it and overcome it. According to Jesus, even mutilation and amputation would be preferable to sin that leads to condemnation. Jesus, while graphic, was not overstating His case.

Sinfulness and hopelessness are related. Sin is not benign or casual; it is neither incidental nor accidental. It is like a cancer that consumes the healthy and strong parts of a person and a society. Sin devastates all it touches, like termites eating silently away within the walls of a house. Sin creates the illusion of freedom as it imprisons and enslaves. Sinfulness is a path that leads to hopelessness.

### Fatal Attraction

The traditional way native Eskimos used to hunt for wolves is a fitting illustration of the seductive and destructive power of sin. *(Let me warn you that this illustration may be too explicit for some. You may want to skip the next two paragraphs.)*

When the Eskimos wanted to kill a wolf, they would take a large knife and coat it with blood. Then they would freeze the knife and apply another coat of blood, allowing that to freeze as well. This process created multiple layers of blood that thoroughly coated the blade. They would then take the knife out to the hunting ground of the wolf and bury the handle in the snow, leaving the blood-coated blade standing erect. Finally, a layer of fresh blood was sprinkled on the frozen blade and on the ground around the standing knife.

A wolf that was drawn to the seductive scent of the fresh blood would begin to lick the frozen blood that coated the knife blade. With each pass of its tongue, the taste of the blood compelled the wolf to lick more vigorously, until the blade of the knife was exposed, cutting the animal. The blood from the knife mingling with the wolf's own blood often increased its desire, causing it to lick with greater frenzy. The result is obvious. Without even realizing it, the wolf would inflict a mortal wound on itself, all the while satisfying its appetite with its own blood.

The image is indeed graphic, but so is the image of a man in pursuit of his own appetites, controlled by sin. The picture of the wolf's suicidal rush to satisfy its appetites ought to bother us, because that is what we are like. Sin is seductive and dangerous. It dangles the bait, sets the hook, and reels us in, often before we know we are caught. To flirt with sin is to play with fire; or as the Eskimo might say, to taste the sin is to lick the knife.

## THE MAGNET OF SIN

For most of us, this is not new news. We know that sin is serious. The question for most of us is not whether sin is serious, but whether or not we are serious about sin.

What do we do about it?

How do we stay "sin-less" in a "sin-full" world?

How do we resist the magnet of sin when our hearts are scrap metal?

Is there anything we can do when the attraction of sin is increasingly unavoidable?

If we live in a cesspool of sin, what hope do we have to come through life smelling like a righteous rose?

What hope do we have to avoid and to overcome the death grip of sin?

## THE HOLY SPIRIT ENABLES
## RADICAL OBEDIENCE

*Therefore, brothers, we have an obligation—but it is not to the sinful nature, to live according to it.*

In Romans 8:12, the first tip to avoiding sin is expressed in the word *obligation*. This is a contractual, legal term that literally means "debt." Therefore, the first key to radical obedience is to stop paying on a debt to our sinful nature—the voice from the past we are no longer obligated to obey.

We do not normally make payments on credit cards we do not own. Apart from some philanthropic project, we do not make payments on someone else's cards. When the credit card company says we owe them nothing, we are typically more than happy to pay them nothing. It is wonderful to hear that you do not have to obey the voice of debt anymore.

### LIVING DEBT FREE

For many of us temptation does not avoid us; it seems to seek us out. It is all around us, assaulting us at every opportunity. Since our culture's economy is built on sin and temptation, we should not be surprised when living obediently is difficult. Neither should we be surprised to find ourselves often face to face with temptation. If we desire to do what is right, how do we handle these frequent confrontations?

Too often we cry out to God for strength even as we run headlong after sin. We ask God to stop us from disobedience as we are in pursuit of it, and then we wonder why He failed us. We lead ourselves into temptation and then whine that God does nothing to get us out.

The hopeful promise of Romans 8:12-13 implies that our obligation is to the Holy Spirit. It is when we obey Him that we are fulfilling our obligation to Him. The strength comes not in our resistance but in our obedience. To put it very simply, we avoid disobedience *by obedience*. When we are doing what is right, we are avoiding what is wrong. Fill your life with righteousness to make less room for unrighteousness. It is when we turn *from* sin that the Holy Spirit gives us strength *not* to sin.

### THE MAN OF STEEL

In the book of Genesis we meet one of the few significant characters in the Bible about whom nothing negative is recorded. His name is

Joseph. If we want some insight into doing the right thing and avoiding the wrong things in life, he seems to be a worthy example.

We are never told the name of Potiphar's wife, but we know a great deal about her character. Joseph was a servant in Potiphar's house, and he was around the house all day. It did not take long before Potiphar's wife noticed this young, handsome, well-built Israelite. After a time she made the kind of play for young Joseph that would make most Hollywood screenwriters proud. Her predatory attitude was as subtle as a howitzer in a bowling alley as she asked Joseph to come to bed with her.[3]

In his refusal, Joseph told this Middle Eastern vixen of his obligation to obey the master of his house, who just so happened to be her husband. Joseph also made plain his own priorities in telling her that he was unwilling to disobey God. Undaunted by his response, she continued to make herself available to him day after day.[4]

Finally, this ongoing soap opera came to its conclusion. Everything in the scriptural account seems to indicate that Joseph walked into this situation completely unaware. As he entered the house, Potiphar's wife threw herself at him and grabbed at his clothes. While this scenario has been repeated endlessly in the name of "entertainment," only rarely has it ended as it did in Genesis 39—Joseph dropped his coat and ran for his life.[5]

## AS THE PHARAOH TURNS

How is it that Joseph was able to withstand the daily suggestions of this temptress?

Was his willpower that much stronger than that of the average male?

Did he lack normal desires?

Was he so holy that he did not even feel the temptation?

Was he hormonally challenged?

Was she just incredibly homely?

I think not.

Joseph's resistance and his obedience are certainly extraordinary but not unattainable. Even though he found himself confronted with constant opportunity to sin, he strengthened his resolve to obey by doing one thing: He kept his distance.

In Genesis 39:10 it says that Joseph *"refused to go to bed with her or even be with her."* In verse 12, as the woman grabbed his clothes, it says, *"he left his cloak in her hand and ran out of the house."*[6] For Joseph there was no flirting with flirting or hanging around with temptation. He kept away, and when that was insufficient, he ran away.

In our struggle to obey, we must understand that we no longer have to sin. We *cannot* sin. When we busy ourselves with obedience, we leave less opportunity for disobedience. Proximity leads to iniquity. If you never get close to the fire, you'll never get burned. When we keep our distance, when we turn away from temptation, we have the promise that we can escape. We have an obligation, not to obey our old nature, but to obey the Holy Spirit, and this means to keep away from sin and close to God.

> *No temptation has seized you except what is common to man. And God is faithful; he will not let you be tempted beyond what you can bear. But when you are tempted, he will also provide a way out so that you can stand up under it.*[7]

We make a serious mistake if we forget that sin is serious business. It requires a strong commitment to avoid being obligated to it. Jesus Christ has made the commitment to set us free from the power and the penalty of sin. When we are committed to live free from our obligation to sin, the Holy Spirit is equally committed to enable serious obedience.

## THE HOLY SPIRIT EMPOWERS
## SINCERE REPENTANCE

I knew what had happened before they sat down. Had I not known of their problems, their body language would have told me. They sat apart, in chairs not facing each other, never making eye contact, never touching. They actually seemed repelled by each other. They exchanged no pet names and gave no verbal signs of intimacy. The husband was "him" or "he"; the wife was "her" or "she," and at times they spoke as if the other person were not even in the room. No compliments or intimacies were exchanged—only chilled, clinical-sounding pronouns and stabbing pejorative observations.

As they rehearsed the events of the past few years and the struggles of the recent weeks, the wreckage of their relationship seemed too mangled to ever repair. It was like listening to an eyewitness account of a train wreck. We were not sure anyone would survive.

The destruction of this once-secure and thriving marriage was caused by one thing: sin. I did not need to be a licensed, accredited, degreed, experienced psychoanalyst to figure this out. One night with one decision, one mistake was made in a moment of weakness. As a result, these two people would be putting the pieces of their relationship back together for years.

Humpty Dumpty has nothing on a person whose life has been knocked apart by the power of sin. Anyone familiar with the struggle to put relationships, families, and even churches back together after a terrible fall can tell you about it.

As we sat together in my office that afternoon, I realized the overpowering sense of hopelessness that one sinful act had produced. At this point they lacked any hope that what they once had could ever be restored.

## SINFULNESS AND HOPELESSNESS

There is a close connection between hopelessness and sinfulness. When sin controls us, it robs us of our freedom and enslaves us. We feel helpless to escape when we are trapped in an endless struggle with sin. When we find ourselves imprisoned in a pattern of disobedience, it is hard for our hope to survive. There are times when sin seems so pervasive and persuasive that we feel hopeless to fight it. When we are victimized by the sins of others, our sense of hopelessness increases.

The connection between sinfulness and hopelessness is highlighted in the first half of Romans 8:13: *"For if you live according to the sinful nature, you will die."* If the verse ended here, it would be one of the most depressing verses in the Bible. Yet this ugly picture is what I saw in the young couple sitting in my office, describing the ruin of their relationship. It was dying from the blast of a terrorist bomb of disobedience.

Fortunately Romans 8:13 does not end in death; it ends with hope: *"But if by the Spirit you put to death the misdeeds of the body, you will live."* The bomb of sin can be defused, and the plot to destroy our hope can be overthrown, if we *"put to death the misdeeds of the body."* But what does this mean?

## THE POWER OF SINCERE REPENTANCE

Sincere repentance is the key. We know that we will struggle with sin. It is the nature of our nature. But we do not need to lose hope when sin causes us to stumble and fall. We can be restored as we seek forgiveness. We need never lose hope, for we know that restoration is possible.

What does sincere repentance look like? It is obviously not to be taken lightly. Repentance is not simply a spiritual "Excuse me" spoken off the cuff and without thought. Repentance is a change of mind and direction.

### A Clear Demonstration of Humility

Humility has often been wrongly associated with self-pity, poverty, modesty, and chivalry. Humility does not mean that you become an emotional whipping post or a relational doormat. True humility does not require "worm theology" or thinking of yourself as a worthless wretch. True humility, the kind that characterizes sincere repentance, does not mean that we think less of ourselves; it means that we do not think of ourselves at all.

The humility that is a chief characteristic of sincere repentance is demonstrated in our attitude toward others and in our attitude toward God. Philippians 2:6 most clearly portrays this humility as it describes Christ: *"Who, being in very nature God, did not consider equality with God something to be grasped."*

Even though He could have laid claim to "equality with God," He did not. In the name of humility, He did not even hold on to His position of deity. His ability to relinquish His rightful glory is a clear demonstration of true humility.

The type of humility that ought to characterize sincere repentance involves one major component—*letting go*. Letting go of our guilt, of our habits, of our expectations, of our vengeance, of our regrets. True humility means to abandon our agendas and our pride. True humility lets go of self-confidence, self-righteousness, and self-pity. We put to death the deeds of the flesh when we humbly repent. In this there is always hope.

### A Committed Desire for Purity

As the young couple in my office struggled through the wreckage that sin had produced in their relationship, their only hope was that a genuine transformation could take place in their lives. While he had to let go of his habits and his addictions, she had to let go of her anger and her vengeance. Yet even this would not be enough to free them to begin rebuilding their relationship. Things had to change from here on out.

As important as a sincere expression of humility is, there is a second quality equally important for true repentance—*the desire for purity*. Sincere repentance is characterized by turning from sin and by turning to holiness. The desire for holiness allows for an occasional lapse in judgment but not for a loss of a sincere hunger to do what is right.

#### SERIOUSLY SERIOUS

The couple who sat in my office is rebuilding their relationship one day at a time, piece by piece. It is not an easy task, but they are committed to it. The sinfulness of the situation has not robbed them of their hope after all. By the grace of God, it need never rob anyone.

The question is not, "Is sin serious?"

The questions is, "Are we serious about sin?"

# SIX

# The Promise
# of Hope

*. . . because those who are led by the Spirit of God*
*are sons of God.*
*For you did not receive a spirit*
*that makes you a slave again to fear,*
*but you received the Spirit of sonship.*
*And by him we cry, "Abba, Father."*
*The Spirit himself testifies with our spirit*
*that we are God's children.*
*Now if we are children,*
*    then we are heirs—heirs of God*
*    and co-heirs with Christ,*
*    if indeed we share in his sufferings*
*    in order that we may also*
*    share in his glory.*

*Romans 8:14-17*

He was a Christmas baby, but for him life was no gift. Born three days after Christmas in the bitter Romanian winter of 1990, he was an orphan before the end of the year. He was not yet two days old when he was turned over to the state authorities.

His mother was a young, impoverished communal farm laborer from the rural outskirts of Arad, Romania, too young and too poor to be anyone's mother. Their bond was one of simple biology and technical legalities. He never knew the warmth of her embrace or the comfort of her voice. She never knew him as her son or had the chance to imprint her love on his heart. She knew him only long enough to leave him with a name, Alexandru Dorel Stark, but little else.

His striking red hair and big round eyes belied the frailty of his congested and underdeveloped lungs. Officially classified as an orphan, the sickly two-day-old Alexandru was taken from his mother to the pediatric hospital in Arad to be placed alongside forty or fifty other "abandoned" infants who had been taken away from their parents or given away by their parents.

In the tumultuous days following the overthrow of communism in Eastern Europe, a Romanian pediatric hospital was more like a prison facility than a care facility for children. Even the sunlight that managed to seep through the unwashed windows seemed stained.

The children's wards in these Romanian "hospitals" were little more than factory-style warehouse cubicles filled end-to-end with chipped metal cribs aligned on cold, resonating concrete floors. The scarred, yellowing cribs seemed more like cages or miniature prison cells than beds for tiny infants. Within the walls of these medical Alcatrazes, the pungent smell of neglect mingled with the aroma of clinical disinterest. There were no colors—only shades of gray. The orphan's ward of a Romanian pediatric hospital was a portrait of desperation and a masterpiece of hopelessness.

### ALEXANDRU'S WORLD

These abandoned children lived a hopeless twilight existence within the walls of their orphanage home. There were two chances for adoption—slim and none. Their lives lacked both privacy and intimacy. Their relentlessly crowded environment provided them with little or no education, personal attention, or hope. They spent their days in dimly lit rooms and their nights on urine-soaked mattresses, constantly surrounded by countless other hope-hardened orphans. Simple survival and a life of indentured poverty was the best a child like Alexandru could expect. It is a bleak existence to be born without a past and live without the hope of any real future.

This was Alexandru Dorel Stark's world. Should he survive, this would be his home. In this world, frail Alexandru was no more than another crying voice to ignore and another hungry mouth to feed. More nuisance than human, he was of little concern to the overworked nurses. He was fed one-half of a bottle of powdered milk twice a day, changed occasionally, and rarely, if ever, held.

## THE GREAT ESCAPE

In the spring of 1991, Chuck and Susan Blair traveled to Arad, Romania, from their home in Plano, Texas. They had heard about the hopeless conditions of orphans in Romania. Their decision to adopt seemed instantaneous, and with only six weeks of research and preparation, they put their lives on hold and set off halfway around the world.

As days turned into weeks, the Blairs found their every hope frustrated. They spent seemingly endless days in frustration, waiting for such things as gasoline or the proper papers or some petty bureaucrat's permission to speak to the proper authorities. They struggled through countless hours trying to untangle the red tape of communist Romanian bureaucracy. Each day they prayed, and they waited, and they prayed, and they waited, and they prayed.

With their window of opportunity beginning to close, late on a Friday afternoon Susan Blair was secretly slipped up to the orphan's wing of the pediatric hospital in Arad. As she entered the first ward through a back stairway, the first child she saw was the frail redhead, Alexandru Dorel Stark. He was underweight, wheezing, and sickly, but to Susan he was the most beautiful boy she had ever seen. No one pressed him into her arms; there was no one trying to sell him to her. There in the clinical starkness of Alexandru's hopeless world, hope had arrived in the form of an American woman.

## THE MIRACLE OF HOPE

Within one month Benjamin Graham Blair was sleeping comfortably in the luxury of his own bed in his own room in his new home in Plano, Texas. His passport and immigration papers showed him to be the son of Charles and Susan Blair. He had become an American citizen with all the rights and privileges of his new birth. His name and his fate were no longer that of a Romanian communal worker but that of a young Texan. His future was no longer confined to the prison of hopelessness but opened to the unlimited opportunities of freedom. He was a legal heir, a free citizen, a son. With their decision to make him their son, Chuck and Susan Blair gave him a new life, a life filled with hope.

When Alexandru Dorel Stark became Benjamin Graham Blair, he became so completely. He became the son of Charles and Susan Blair for better or for worse, for richer or for poorer, for life. He did not become some disposable appendage or temporary houseguest but a permanent, lifelong, full-fledged son.

Chuck and Susan understood that, as a condition of his adoption, Ben would be their son for life. It was a permanent deal. Because of this, Ben permanently has all the rights and privileges as a legal heir of his new parents. He is no longer a citizen of Romania, but of America. And should he ever doubt any of this, all he has to do is check the record.

This, however, is not just the story of a tiny Romanian infant. This is *our* story. As it is for Alexandru, so it is for those of us who are called the children of God.

## THE BELIEVER'S BIRTH CERTIFICATE

You could call Romans 8:14-17 the Believer's Birth Certificate, the Christian's Certificate of Adoption. In these four compact verses we have the binding legal promise of our eternal adoption. This passage guarantees our position as sons and daughters, with all rights and privileges. We are citizens of heaven, children of God by our new birth.

In one of Paul's finest hours, he penned Romans 8:14-17 to highlight the wonder of our adoption. In so doing, he entered into the written record four promises of God to all those who are His children.

## THE PROMISE OF GUIDANCE

The first promise of our adoption is that those who are the sons of God will be led by the Spirit of God. That is to say, those who have been adopted, those who are God's children will be guided in their lives and in their decisions by the Spirit of God. This is both the promise and the proof of a true relationship with God.

But how do we know if we are being led by the Spirit of God?

What does it mean to be led by the Spirit of God?

How do we know when we are being led by the spirit of something or someone else?

These are critical questions, since this leading is supposed to happen to all who are the authentic children of God.

## GETTING THE LEAD OUT

We can be certain that being led by the Spirit of God does *not* mean being led into disobedience. God does not lead anyone to sin. You can be pretty sure that the Spirit is not leading you to commit murder so that you can start a prison ministry. Likewise, the Spirit is not the one guiding you to rob a bank so that you can give more money to missions.

We know that the Spirit would not lead us to do things contradictory to His Word. It is a fairly safe bet that God is not leading you to divorce your spouse, abuse your children, disrespect your parents, or stop attending church so that you can watch more football. Anything that cannot be affirmed by God's Word or that contradicts God's Word is not the leading of the Spirit. God has never been in the habit of contradicting Himself; he's not about to start with you.

### The Cosmic Cowboy

I am also convinced that being led by the Spirit does not normally involve coercion. He does not lead us as you would lead a stubborn mule. This is not to say that we do not sometimes behave like stubborn mules, but rather that God does not regularly lead us this way. He does not habitually use the "Rawhide" method of leading us through life: "Don't try to understand 'em; just ride and rope and brand 'em." He is not a cowboy; He is a shepherd.

While God can and does at times lead His children with a pillar of fire, a talking mule, or a voice from heaven, this is not the norm. If Romans 8:14 means that only those led in this way are the children of God, then my guess is that few of us could claim sonship. For most of us, the only pillar of fire we have seen before the people of God is at a church picnic, and our only experience with the handwriting on the wall involves crayons and two-year-olds.

## The Great Shepherd

Being led by the Spirit *does* mean being led to do some things that we are not naturally inclined to do, even being led to do things we may resist. However, even in these cases, it does not mean that the Spirit drags us kicking and screaming. He leads us; He does not push, force, or manipulate us.

He leads His people like a shepherd. It has been said that you can no more drive sheep than you can push a rope uphill. Sheep must be led. Sometimes the shepherd carries the sheep. Sometimes the shepherd rescues the sheep. Sometimes the shepherd prods the sheep with his staff, but he rarely drives them like cattle.

To be led by the Spirit of God, as the children of God, is to be led by the Great Shepherd. A shepherd moves his sheep gradually from pasture to pasture. He occasionally uses his rod and his staff, but even these tools are a "comfort" to his sheep. He cares for and stands with his sheep whether they are beside quiet waters, in the presence of their enemies, or in the valley of the shadow of death.

## Hurry Up and Slow Down

I understand this to mean that if you are in a hurry, filled with anxiety and fear; if you have no comfort or peace about what you are doing; if the decisions you are making are "far afield," "way out there," or just so radically different from where God has led you up to this point, then you should be very careful about your choices. Ask yourself if that is how a shepherd would lead you. A cowboy maybe, a shepherd never.

When you sense His presence, when everything seems to be consistent with where God has placed you up to this time, when you can recognize and accept the purpose and lessons of His rod and staff, then it is a good bet that you are being led by the Great Shepherd.

There are plenty of cowboys out there who want you to be part of their herd. But don't be confused. In His presence there is peace, not a stampede. God is a God of peace, not of confusion. It is probably wise to assume that when the crowd's charging off in a different direction, it's possibly not the work of the Great Shepherd but of spiritual rustlers. The shepherd does not lead by majority vote. When everybody else is running along with the herd, be careful. God just may not be going that way.

### 20/20 Hindsight

Look back over the pathways of your life.

Where have you come from?

Do you see the shepherding of God in your life?

Can you spot His fingerprints on your decisions and provisions?

All those who are His children can. Just as clearly as young Ben can see how his life was changed by the care of Chuck and Susan Blair, so too the child of God can see the evidence in his life of God's transforming care. This is how we know the Spirit of God has been and is guiding us.

### IN HIS STEPS

We also know that the leading of the Spirit follows in the footsteps of Jesus. If you are going where Jesus would not go, doing what Jesus would not do, saying what Jesus would not say (write this down in ink; carve it in granite), He is not the one leading you.

To follow Him is to follow His example. To be led by Him is to follow His Word, to keep His commandments. If we know that the Spirit does not lead us to disobey, to sin, or to do what is contradictory to His Word, then we also know that the Spirit *does* lead us to obey, to avoid sin, and to do what we are instructed to do in His Word.

### WORKING WITHOUT A NET

The Lord certainly enjoys drawing outside our lines and working without a net. There is no denying that He can and does use extraordinary means to lead His people. However, the promise of Romans 8:14 is not that God will provide sporadic supernatural communiqués to authenticate that we are His children.

The promise of Romans 8:14 is more like the promise of Chuck to Benjamin Blair: Every day you will be able to look around you and see the affirmation of your adoption. This means that those who are God's children will be continuously led by His Spirit and that this leading will be a consistent and visible characteristic of their lives. Those who are the children of God seek to follow in the footsteps of the Great Shepherd *daily*, not just occasionally.

Consider the wisdom of Proverbs 3:5-6: *"Trust in the* LORD *with all your heart and lean not on your own understanding; in all your ways acknowledge him, and he will make your paths straight."* The promise to the children of God has always been the same: If you are His children, He will lead you. The authentication of God's children is the same as it always was: If He leads you, you are His sons. The first promise to those who are called the children of God is the promise of guidance. It is a birthright and a birthmark.

## THE PROMISE OF INTIMACY

Romans 8:15 promises, *"For you did not receive a spirit that makes you a slave again to fear, but you received the Spirit of sonship. And by him we cry, 'Abba, Father.'"*

As a kid I hated to be called names. No matter how innocent they were, they always seemed hurtful or mean. Whether they were twisted anatomical references or slanderous mispronunciations of my family name, they always hurt my feelings so that I found them hard to ignore. Sticks and stones never did break any of my bones, but names did hurt me. If you wanted my attention—or my anger—on the school playground, all you had to do was call me a name.

### PATTY-MELT

I am still being called names. Some, I am thankful, I never hear. Others I hear quite often—honey, Daddy, Reverend, Pastor, Sir, Doctor, Mr. Haney, and so forth. While I am comfortable with all of these names, they hold neither the significance nor the affection of one special name—"Patty-melt."

"Patty-melt" is not some romantic pet name my wife gave me. (Although I do like patty-melt sandwiches, I am not sure how romantic the name is.) Nor is "Patty-melt" a commentary on my terrible eating habits and my middle-age weight problems. "Patty-melt" is a private name that only my daughters use. It is a distant relation to the term "Daddy," personalized over time through my daughters' constant rhyming (daddy/patty).

For anyone else to refer to me as a greasy, onion-covered, toasted cheese and hamburger sandwich would be an insult. But knowing my children's affectionate intent, the name "Patty-melt," when spoken by them, will always be a compliment. The name is special only because of the relationship.

## THE RIGHT OF RELATIONSHIP

All of us understand the nature of these pet names and nicknames. We have them for special friends and relatives. Husbands and wives often give each other absurd and even somewhat insulting handles such as "my little dumpling," "baby-cakes," and so forth. We all know that in a loving relationship, various references to food groups, small animals, and incomprehensible babble can serve as intimate communication. Grandparents the world over receive with delight all manner of odd-sounding names from their grandchildren.

### Our Heavenly Dad

Romans 8:15 is the second provision of our adoption as God's children. We are given permission to call Him "Daddy." This is a privilege afforded *only* to those who are His children. To call the Creator of the heavens and the earth, the King of all Kings and the Lord of all Lords, the Ruler and Sustainer of the universe a pet name is either a right of relationship and an indication of intimacy, or it is blasphemy.

When Jesus dared to identify the God of Abraham, Isaac, and Jacob as His father, the religious leaders of His day sought to have Him stoned to death.[1] On another occasion, Jesus defended His sonship, identifying God as the source of His miracles and calling Him Father. Once again the implication of this kind of intimacy with God drew cries of blasphemy from the religious leaders of Jesus' day, and they again called for the stones.[2]

It is no small thing to call God our Father, and it is only His children who can even think of calling Him "Daddy." This is the most personal reference to God that any creature can make. The significance of this relationship is underscored in Galatians 4:6-7: *"Because you are sons, God sent the Spirit of his Son into our hearts, the Spirit who calls out, 'Abba, Father.' So you are no longer a slave, but a son; and since you are a son, God has made you also an heir."*

## The Freedom of Fatherhood

This intimate privilege is the promise of Romans 8:15. This is the promise of the freedom of fatherhood, the promise of intimacy with God. When we feel hopeless and helpless, we are guaranteed as His children to have a special relationship with Him.

This is not a *slave/master* relationship, but a *father/son* relationship. The quality of this relationship frees us *for* intimacy with God, and this intimacy frees us *from* the fear that comes from a conditional, works-oriented, master/slave relationship. We are free from fear and free for intimacy. This is the promise of His presence. The freedom *for* intimacy is the promise of freedom *from* fear. This is the promise and the instruction of 1 John 4:15-18:

> *If anyone acknowledges that Jesus is the Son of God, God lives in him and he in God. And so we know and rely on the love God has for us. God is love. Whoever lives in love lives in God, and God in him. In this way, love is made complete among us so that we will have confidence on the day of judgment, because in this world we are like him.* There is no fear in love. But perfect love drives out fear, because fear has to do with punishment. The man who fears is not made perfect in love [emphasis mine].

## The Father's Ear

From the moment young Ben Blair could speak, he had the right to call Chuck Blair Daddy. As his son, Ben can call Chuck by a name reserved only for his children. This is his legal right. It is the promise of his adoption.

At a crowded ball game or at any event where the confusing din of voices fills the air, all Ben has to do to get his father's undivided attention is to cry out, "Hey, Dad!" And as any parent will tell you, that familiar call will rise above the blanket of noise and reach his father's ears. It is the power and the privilege of sonship.

Consider for a moment the Father's perspective. Not only is a father specially attuned to hear his child's voice, but the sound of that voice can also bring him great pleasure. To hear the familiar call of "Dad!" from among the crowd goes directly to his heart. Almost instantly a father can discern a greeting from a warning, a cry for help from a call for attention, a request from a demand. Above the noise, in the midst of a crowd, a father can tell all this just from the one word *Dad.*

## THE PROMISE OF ASSURANCE

Romans 8:16 sets forth the third promise of our adoption: *"The Spirit himself testifies with our spirit that we are God's children."*

What then is the content of the Spirit's testimony written on our spirit?

How does the Spirit bear witness?

What exactly is the testimony of the Holy Spirit?

Can you hear it?

Can you feel it?

What does it sound like?

If we are to build our hope on this testimony, we ought to know what this means.

If you were on trial for being a Christian, would there be enough evidence to convict you? Romans 8:16 indicates that the believer has not only enough evidence for conviction, but evidence *of* conviction in his life.

### THE LIFE OF A MARTYR

The key word in this verse is συμμαρτυρέω (*summartureo*)[3] This compound word is only used by Paul in the book of Romans (2:15, 8:16, and 9:1), and in each of these contexts, the force of the word is directly related to a person's visible actions and conscience. The eventual usage of the root word μαρτυρέω (*martureo*) came to describe one who had sacrificed his or her life for the cause of Christ (*martyr*). This usage highlights the underlying correlation between conscience and actions.

However, the word μαρτυρέω (*martureo*) also has legal overtones. In the context of a court of law, the Holy Spirit provides the evidence that, when examined by the jury of our spirit, it is sufficient to convince us of our relationship with the Father. This testimony, or witness, much as in a court of law, involves both circumstantial evidence and eyewitness testimony.

### Exhibit A: The Testimony of the Logos

Tucked away in a safe place is the documentation that assures Benjamin Blair of his birthright as the son of Chuck and Susan Blair. Documents from the Immigration and Naturalization Service, the State Department, the Government of Romania, the Department of Health and Human Services, and various legal documents from the State of Texas form a pile of certainty for young Ben. This is legal proof according to all national and international laws. Should anyone, including Ben himself, ever question his relationship, his freedom, his rights, or his adoption, he has a mountain of legal evidence to back his claims.

As adopted children of God, we believers not only have the promise of Romans 8 but also countless other scriptural documents upon which we secure our case for our right of relationship with God. The Spirit of God could be considered to be the author of the Word of God. Therefore we could consider His testimony in the Word to be a witness with our spirit that we are the children of God.

This documentation extends all the way back to the first book of the Bible, in which God promised his servant Abraham that one day all the nations of the earth would be blessed through him.[4] This scarlet thread of the parent/child relationship between God and His people is tightly woven through the words of the psalmists, the prophets, the poets, and the historians of the Old Testament. Jesus Himself consistently validated the father/son relationship that was available to those who enter into a relationship with Him. The writings of each of the New Testament authors provide consistent affirmation of the believer's birthright. Even in the final chapters of the Word of God, in the book of Revelation, we are given written guarantees of our adoption and our relationship with Him. You could say that from the beginning to the end, we have God's Word on it.

### Exhibit B: The Eyewitness

As if this weren't enough, we believers have an additional affirmation of our relationship with God. According to Romans 8:16, every believer has the testimony of the Holy Spirit supporting our relationship with our heavenly Father. We not only have documented evidence of our relationship with God through His Word, but we also have an eyewitness who is willing to testify concerning our relationship with God.

In any court of law the testimony of a witness is only as valuable as the character of that witness. Almost anyone can say almost anything under the right circumstances. The significance of the testimony of a witness is directly linked to his integrity.

When we are promised in Romans 8:16 that the Holy Spirit testifies with our spirit, we could not possibly have a witness of any higher integrity. We not only have the Word of God as a whole providing the documentation to support our case, but we also have specific words of God in that book testifying in our behalf. The testimony of the Holy Spirit with our spirit also includes those character and personality traits, those habits, priorities, and family traits that are a reflection of our Father.

As young Ben Blair ventures out from his parents' supervision, he will carry within him the testimony of his father. As he makes decisions and choices about life, the patterns, priorities, and values of his dad will influence his choices, sometimes whether he likes it or not. While at times he may choose differently from his father, his father's "voice" will still speak within his mind. His father's opinions will still enter into his decisions. And if psychologists are correct, young Ben Blair will reflect more of old Chuck Blair than he may wish or expect. This is our spirit bearing witness with our father's spirit that we are his children.

### Exhibit C: The Fingerprints of Faith

A number of years ago our church was burglarized. Upon arriving at my office the morning after the crime, I noticed that something was amiss—the church office door was beaten to splinters, and my office door was scarred by the forceful use of a crowbar.

When the police arrived, they called for a crime scene investigator. Some clues were obvious, such as the massacred door and the trail of muddy footprints. Yet it was not these blatant clues that finally identified the perpetrators. What led the police to the burglars was virtually invisible to the naked eye—fingerprints.

As the crime scene investigator worked, he strategically placed a fine graphite dust on the doors and walls. A moment's examination of the dust revealed the previously invisible outline of a person's fingerprint. Once the fingerprints of all the church staff had been eliminated, the investigator was able to identify the prints of our burglars.

This common detective practice is illustrative of how the Holy Spirit leaves evidence of His activity in our lives. Sometimes the evidence is blatant, as when His deep footprints can be seen easily. Yet other times His work is more subtle, even almost invisible. But with careful examination, it is possible to discern His work from our own and to see His fingerprints on our lives.

For all of us who are the children of God, these fingerprints will exist. They are the testimony of the Spirit's work in our lives. His Spirit does testify with our spirit that we are the children of God, and every believer can find enough evidence for a conviction.

## THE PROMISE OF INHERITANCE

*Now if we are children, then we are heirs—heirs of God and co-heirs with Christ, if indeed we share in his sufferings in order that we may also share in his glory. (Romans 8:17)*

### THE FAMILY FARM

My parents now make their home on our family farm in northeastern Pennsylvania. This farm has been in my family since just after the Civil War. I have roamed its cornfields and climbed up its slate-covered hills from the time I could first walk. My great-grandfather built the house my parents now live in, and my grandfather built the barn. This place is more than a piece of property; it is a legacy.

Late one summer night a couple of years ago, I woke my daughters up and took them in their pajamas up the hill behind my parents' home. It was a warm night, and moon shadows accompanied us up the hill.

Without responding to their sleepy pleas for an explanation, I led them to the small summit behind the house and pointed toward the southern horizon. There in the distance, silently signaling from above the silhouetted tree-lined ridge, was a fiery thunderstorm. Its orange-white electrical fury danced within the translucent cocoon of the towering clouds. The jagged strobes flashed like fireworks behind a distant gray curtain, too far away for us to hear, but close enough for us to admire its wonder and power.

I then turned the girls around and told them to look to the north, to the distant hill that leaned against the unclouded horizon. Then I had them look to the west and to the east, pointing out the boundaries of the farm that were cut into the sky by a serrated line of trees.

Then I looked down at my three precious daughters and said, "Girls, look at the storms in the south, the stars in the north, the trees in the west, and the trees in the east—from this hill to that ridge and from that storm to that hill." My hands conducted their visual tour. "All of this is your inheritance."

As they rubbed their eyes and gazed in all directions, I continued in a mythic tone, "Over 100 years before you were born, your great-great-grandfather may have stood on this very hill on a night just like this and looked up at those stars and hills and trees surrounding his family farm. Even though you did not know him, he left all of this for you—not because of anything you've ever done but because you are his heirs, his descendants."

### Heirs of Hope

As believers we have the promise of a glorious inheritance, one far better than a few acres of farmland. We are promised an inheritance that will never spoil or fade, a place of peace and rest, a place within the Father's house where He will wipe away every tear from our eyes. We are promised the inheritance of eternal life. We are heirs of the hope of heaven.

Whether or not we live worthy of this inheritance, as His children we are the only ones who can lay claim to it. We are heirs not because of anything we have done, but because of who we are related to. We are heirs not because of who we are, but because of whose we are.

Ours is a promise of birth, a reward for being born into a family. According to Romans 8:17, we are the heirs of God, the inheritors of eternal life, of heaven, and of the righteousness of Christ. This inheritance has been bought, paid for, and bequeathed to all those who are in His family.

When all of our resources are depleted and we are struggling to find hope, we should remember the legacy of hope we have. The hope of a secure homestead. A promised place of peace and rest, of security and certainty. A place bought and paid for in full. Deeded to us as children. As a part of what it means to be His children, we will always have a hope; we will always have our home. We have the assurance of our inheritance; we can never be written out of the will.

### Streets of Gold and Callused Hands

When I was eighteen years old, my uncle and my father sat me down at the kitchen table in my grandparents' farmhouse. I had just spent the better part of my summer working around the farm—putting up walls, roofing buildings, and mowing grass. My uncle and my father wanted to let me know that even though they appreciated my help around the farm, this was simply my responsibility as a member of the family. All this work was part of the deal. The farm, including its labor, would be my inheritance. You see, there is a downside to inheriting a family farm—commonly called *hard work*.

Even though our eternal inheritance is secured without our hard work, owning such an inheritance often requires that we work hard. No inheritance is without its share of difficulties. There is more to being a child of God than streets of gold and angelic choirs. There are some blisters and bruises to be had along the way.

### Sitting at the Kitchen Table

Paul passed this wisdom on to his young protégé Timothy just before his death. In 2 Timothy 3:10-12 Paul has the "kitchen-table" conversation with the one who would inherit the glory and pain of Paul's ministry:

> *You, however, know all about my teaching, my way of life, my pur-*
> *pose, faith, patience, love, endurance, persecutions, sufferings—*
> *what kinds of things happened to me in Antioch, Iconium and*
> *Lystra, the persecutions I endured. Yet the Lord rescued me from*
> *all of them.* In fact, everyone who wants to live a godly life in
> Christ Jesus will be persecuted [emphasis mine].

Peter also sits with us at the "kitchen table." For he knew well the bumps in the road to our inheritance. In 1 Peter 4:12-14 he lets us know of the struggles this side of heaven:

> *Dear friends, do not be surprised at the painful trial you are suf-*
> *fering, as though something strange were happening to you. But*
> *rejoice that you participate in the sufferings of Christ, so that you*
> *may be overjoyed when his glory is revealed. If you are insulted*
> *because of the name of Christ, you are blessed, for the Spirit of*
> *glory and of God rests on you.*

We ought not be surprised when the inheritance includes some hard times, for even the Master, Jesus Himself, predicted a tough row to hoe as He sits with us at the "kitchen table" in John 15:18-21:

> *"If the world hates you, keep in mind that it hated me first. If you*
> *belonged to the world, it would love you as its own. As it is, you*
> *do not belong to the world, but I have chosen you out of the world.*
> *That is why the world hates you. Remember the words I spoke to*
> *you: 'No servant is greater than his master.' If they persecuted me,*
> *they will persecute you also. If they obeyed my teaching, they will*
> *obey yours also. They will treat you this way because of my name,*
> *for they do not know the One who sent me."*

To be an heir is a marvelous thing. It means that we have something in store for us that we did not earn, do not deserve, and could not purchase. But the reality of being an heir also means that in this life we have to "work the farm." The blessings of our inheritance include a definite responsibility with a definite downside.

But imagine for a minute life without the assurance of this inheritance—the same amount of work, the same amount of trials, the same number of blisters and calluses, and yet no hope. If you ask me, I'll put up with the sweat and dirt of this life, for I know it does not even compare with the inheritance I will one day receive.

## THE FAMILY FORTUNE

Chuck Blair laughs when I mention the "family fortune" to which Ben is entitled. The Rockefellers or Perots they are not, but compared to Ben's natural family in Arad, Romania, the Blairs own the world. However, Ben is not simply an heir of the property of Charles and Susan Blair. He is also an heir of their real fortune—their legacy. As a son, he is entitled to the most valuable asset passed down from Chuck's grandfather to his father to him—his family.

To be an heir of a true family fortune means that we never have to face the trials of life alone. The most precious inheritance is the inheritance of love and hope. The real jewels in the family crown are the unconditional relationships of moms and dads, brothers and sisters, grandparents and grandchildren. In a world where everyone else will place limitations on their loyalty, a genuine family is a place of grace. The real heirloom for young Ben is the refuge of mercy and forgiveness in a loving family, a harbor in the storms of life to come.

The greatest danger for those of us in the family of God is not insecurity; it is apathy. We might take our miraculous adoption for granted. Ours is not a problem of boasting but of coasting. Yet the evidence of the Word of God and in virtually every dimension of our lives testifies to the miracle of the hope we have.

## THE FAMILY OF HOPE

As Chuck and Susan Blair made their way through the Romanian maze of bribes and red tape and interviewed Alexandru's birth mother, they made a miraculous discovery. They found that 200 miles northeast of Arad, there was a small redheaded fourteen-month-old girl named Dorinna Roxanna Stark—Ben's sister. She too had been incarcerated in an orphanage prison facing an identical life of hopelessness. Even though the odds of them ever meeting were infinitely small, they were brother and sister by more than physical birth—by destiny.

To adopt one Romanian child required a near-miraculous chain of events, near the equivalent of winning the lottery. Not only did all of the legal requirements (which changed at a moment's notice) have to be met, but every unwritten and unspoken contingency had to be planned for, paid off, or properly dealt with. Attempting to adopt a second child did not make this process twice as hard; it made it one thousand times as difficult. This would be the same as winning the lottery—without buying a ticket.

Chuck and Susan will gladly tell you what they have told their children: It was only because of God's amazing work that Ben and Katy managed to become Blairs. There is no doubt in their minds that His hand was guiding them through the process. Ben and his sister Katy will live their lives staring in the face of a miracle.

## THIS IS OUR STORY

Ben came to his new home with more than new parents; he came into an entire family. Not only did he come to a new life with a new sister, but one year later Susan Blair gave birth to twin boys, Matt and Sam. Benjamin Blair has been given a life with a sister he had never known, in a country he had never seen, with a mother and a father he could not have imagined, with two brothers even his parents did not expect.

The transformation is complete. While he was born a lonely, hopeless orphan, a child born in another land, he will grow up in the midst of a lively family as a brother and a son.

But this is not just the story of a young Romanian boy; this is our story. This is our hope, our inheritance, our birthright. The transformation, the provision, the family, and the miracle of hope are for those of us in the family of God—as real and as powerful as it is for Ben and Katy Blair. While we may not always feel like or act like His children, and while we may fail to appreciate the fullness of our adoption each and every moment, our hope will never, ever change.

We have His Word on it.

# SEVEN

# The Struggle of Hope

I consider that our present sufferings
  are not worth comparing with
  the glory
  that will be revealed in us.
The creation waits in eager expectation
  for the sons of God to be revealed.
  For the creation was subjected to frustration,
  not by its own choice,
  but by the will of the one who subjected it,
  in hope that
  the creation itself will be liberated
  from its bondage to decay
  and brought into
  the glorious freedom
  of the children of God.
We know that
  the whole creation has been groaning
  as in the pains of childbirth
  right up to the present time.
Not only so,
  but we ourselves,
  who have the firstfruits of the Spirit,
  groan inwardly
  as we wait eagerly for our adoption as sons,
  the redemption of our bodies.

*For in this hope we were saved.*
*But hope that is seen*
*is no hope at all.*
*Who hopes for what he already has?*
*But if we hope for what we do not yet have,*
*we wait for it patiently.*

*Romans 8:18-25*

A number of years ago my younger brother Peter was accused of sexual misconduct with a two-year-old boy. Even though the horrifying accusations were completely false, their impact was devastating, creating an emotional and spiritual firestorm that engulfed every area of his life.

On the day these startling accusations were made, my brother called me on the phone and said, "The only thing of real value to me in my life is my reputation and my integrity. And now they have been taken away." His broken heart and wounded spirit were communicated halfway across the country to me as clearly as his voice.

For most of the evening he expressed his pain and bewilderment over such absurd, outrageous charges. Based solely on the garbled utterances of a two-year-old, the accusations jeopardized my brother's career, mangled his confidence, destroyed his reputation, and besieged his faith. Not only had a family whose friendship he cherished brought these charges, but also many whose confidence he had relied on were now questioning his integrity and behavior.

To be sure, accusations of this kind have to be taken seriously even if they are later found to be baseless. The painful reality of the times in which we live turned the monosyllabic comments of a small child into a whirlwind of agony for Peter. Police interviews, psychological profiles, legal discussions, suspicions, and suspensions filled most of the next year. For a young man who had devoted the better part of his life to sacrificial ministry for God, these events smacked of theistic betrayal.

### RIPPING HOLES IN OUR HOPE

How could God possibly allow this kind of thing to happen to someone whose very life is a model of spiritual commitment and self-sacrifice?

Of all of the troubles that could possibly enter his life, why did God allow one that so devastated the most valuable possession in his life, his reputation?

If it is hard to suffer the consequences of our own iniquities and stupidities, it is all the more brutal to suffer when we are innocent and we find ourselves abandoned and defenseless.

## SPIRITUAL BAND-AIDS ON GAPING WOUNDS

At this point theologians, pastors, authors, and well-intentioned counselors rush in where even angels fear to tread. They bring with them biblical Band-Aids and salves mixed with bits of wisdom from Job and shallow observations from the sufferings of Jesus. Too often well-meaning friends and advisors gush biblical psychobabble that soothes a suffering soul about as well as brine in an open wound. If we are honest, we must admit that none of these easy "answers" seems to suffice. In times such as these there are no easy answers, and the only adequate comfort is sympathetic silence.

We all know what it means to lift our eyes to heaven, asking through gritted teeth, "Why me? Why now? Why this? Why, God?" and find the only response from heaven is a holy silence. The struggle to maintain our hope is shaped in times such as these.

To be sure, the fabric of our lives is woven with occasional and unpredictable strands of barbed wire, and as we wrap ourselves in the cloth of time, we all experience unexpected pain. From the most tragic of injustices to the sting of self-inflicted wounds, each of us comes in contact with suffering. From time to time each of us asks the unanswerable question, "Why me?" Times like these frustrate our faith, limit our love—and may even rip holes in the fabric of our hope.

## MAROONED ON A MUTINOUS PLANET

God never underestimates suffering. The Bible never invalidates the reality of pain. In fact, the opposite is true: The Word of God is filled with images of suffering innocents, broken and bruised heroes, floods of injustice and iniquity, and a Savior as its centerpiece who knew first-hand the brutality of a hurting and hurtful world. As Philip Yancey says, "We are marooned on a mutinous planet."[1] And we are all victimized by the rebellion.

Although we live in a world where something is terribly wrong, the message of God to us in times of pain is not a critical or condemning one but an empathetic and compassionate one. To those of us asking the unanswerable whys comes a message of hope, spoken by a God who has clothed Himself in the barbed-wire fabric of a sinful world.

## THE REBARS OF HOPE

When I was in college, one of my favorite and best-paying summer jobs was driving a truck for the Lentini family concrete company. This was a very macho thing to do, and it also exposed me to a world of blue-collar wisdom I otherwise may have missed. Knowledge about everything from catering-truck etiquette to the fine art of double-clutching a fifteen-speed Autocar diesel may not seem essential in the everyday world of pastoral ministry, but I am a better man for having it.

One of the secrets of the masonry and concrete trade that I learned very early that summer was the importance of properly placed rebars. *Rebar* is a contractor's term for a steel reinforcing rod. Perhaps you have seen them laid out in a crisscross pattern in a sidewalk, a driveway, or a street before the concrete is poured.

The location, size, and number of rebars placed in a concrete form are not simply determined by "feel"; there are specific engineering requirements and government codes that specify how many are laid where. Improperly placed or incorrectly sized rebars can cause a highway to crack, or worse, a building to collapse. Concrete alone is not strong enough to withstand the loads and stresses of heavy construction; properly placed steel rebars are what give the concrete its real strength.

Romans 8:18-25 strengthens our hope the way rebars strengthen concrete. When these promises are inserted into our lives, even though they may be hidden beneath the surface, they form a steel skeleton that allows us to withstand the twists and stresses of life.

When we are carrying the heavy loads of life, when the pressure bears down on us and presses against us, the promises of Romans

8:18-25 work like rebars of hope. Skillfully placed, laid side by side one right after the other, overlapping and crisscrossing, these four promises are designed to take the stresses, strains, twists, and pressures of the heaviest load. When the accusations are brutal, the questions unanswered, and the injustices crushing, these rebars of hope give real strength to our lives.

## OUR HOPE PUTS OUR PAIN
### IN PERSPECTIVE

*I consider that our present sufferings are not worth comparing with the glory that will be revealed in us. The creation waits in eager expectation for the sons of God to be revealed. (Romans 8:18-19)*

Verses 18 and 19 form the first rebar placed within our lives to give us a sustaining strength. We could call it the rebar of an eternal perspective. Our ability to survive the inevitable trials of life is strengthened when we view them in the light of our eternal hope and our eternal home, heaven.

However, this strength comes from doing more than simply thinking about eternity and heaven. This strength comes from thinking about our life and all of its heartaches in light of heaven and eternity. As our hope is built upon the foundation of eternity, it is only as strong as our grasp of the reality of heaven.

### DRIVING RAIN

In Texas they are called "gully washers" or "toad chokers"—those violent downpours that are so intense there seems to be no space between the drops. A few seconds in one of these mini-monsoons can soak a person through to the bone. It takes only a few minutes for the streets to flood over their curbs and for once-small streams to become raging rivers.

If you ever find yourself driving in one of these torrents, you will notice that your wipers cannot clear the windshield fast enough. There is not a "deluge" setting after "fast" on most car wiper systems. Even the fastest setting often fails to keep up. Being on the road in one of these cloudbursts can give a new meaning to the term "driving rain."

## Watching the Wipers

We all know that when you drive, it is best not to watch the wipers. The general idea is to look past the wipers and out to the road ahead of you. To focus on the wipers, no matter how bad the deluge, is always a bad idea. This is not an advanced concept; this is Drivers' Ed. Common Sense 101.

Why then do we live our lives focusing on the wipers? I understand that at times the downpour of trials is so heavy and the rain of pain is so intense that we cannot see beyond the next few feet. Still this never means that we should take our eyes off of where we are going and stare at the struggling wipers directly in front of us. Why is it that when the pain of life grows so intense, like a deluge, that we abandon what we know to be true and right? Why do we take our eyes off of the road ahead and become obsessed with only what is directly in our view?

## The Mathematics of Eternity

Romans 8:18 does not deny the reality of these storms, nor it is meant to devalue the suffering and pain in this life; on the contrary, this verse validates it. For according to Romans 8:18, if we could possibly calculate all of the pain and suffering in the entire world—from the hunger pangs of a starving infant to the death heaves of a dying grandfather—and multiply all of these by all of the tragedies and trials ever faced by everyone who has ever lived, and add to this each person's individual hurts and fears, both small and great, and then achieve a sum total value of all of the suffering of all of mankind through all of history, it would not begin to compare with the joy and the peace and the glory of heaven.

This implies that in the mathematics of eternity, the total of all of our personal struggles will not exceed the sum of our joy in heaven. Even when we believe we are drowning in a bottomless sea of grief, this apparent endlessness cannot compare with what waits for us in eternity. From the smallest hangnail to the greatest heartache, their sum total will not begin to fill the depths of heaven or cover the length of eternity.

ETERNITY = MESS$^2$. This is the mathematics of eternity, the formula of Romans 8:18: *"I consider that our present sufferings are not worth comparing with the glory that will be revealed in us."* When the struggles of life don't make sense and the injustices seem to be endless, when nothing in life seems to "add up"—that is the point. In the Mathematics of Hope, the greater the total of all of the pain and suffering of this life, the greater our assurance of the total of peace and joy of heaven, for the latter will always exceed the former. If it doesn't seem to "add up," remember that without an eternal perspective, in this life, it never will.

THE GLORY IN US. It is easy for us to overlook the small preposition at the end of verse 18 and move on to the next verse—after all, it is only two letters. Even though the word is easy to miss, we should not ignore its implications.

The glory that will be revealed will certainly be revealed "to" us when we get to heaven. However, this is not the limit of the nature of this glory; it is not simply a glory that is "for" us. This simple preposition also implies that this glory will be revealed "by" us or "in" us when we get to heaven. We will not just be the audience of God's glory; we will be the principal agents of God's glory.

This means that as we look around the corridors of heaven and search through the reaches of eternity, the glory of our redemption will be the most spectacular aspect of heaven. Of all the creatures and all the magnificent creation that we will enjoy in eternity, the greatest instrument of God's glory will be ourselves. As we are reunited with those we love, as we see the lives of those who have been touched by our own, as we travel throughout heaven, His glory will be revealed not only to us but also by us. We are the agents and the audience of God's glory.

## CREATION ON TIPTOE

With this in mind, Paul adds to our eternal perspective as he says, *"The creation waits in eager expectation for the sons of God to be revealed."* All of creation is anticipating the moment when we, the agents of God's glory, will be revealed.

"Eager expectation" is a marvelous word picture of the state of anticipation in which all of creation now finds itself. The first of the two words used here literally means "to stretch one's head out."[2] This depicts someone "stretching his neck" to see over a crowd of people, searching to see someone or something in the distance. This is also the image of a runner straining forward with all of the body at the finish line in order to win. J. B. Phillips in his translation of the New Testament poetically renders it as creation standing on tiptoes.

### Living in the State of Anticipation

This is the state of all of creation, a state of anticipation. But anticipation of what? The creation is waiting with focused intent for one event: "for the sons of God to be revealed." This implies that we do not yet realize all that we will one day be in Christ. The fullness of what it means to be a child of God is still hidden from creation and from us. While we may already have a glimpse of what it means to be redeemed as we fellowship among and behold the body of Christ on earth, we have yet to see it in its fullness.

The implication of this anticipation gives me hope, for I know that it will ultimately be God who will sort the "sons of God" out. We often spend considerable energy and anxiety trying to assure ourselves of the salvation of others. While we must be aggressive in our proclamation of the Gospel, it is not up to us to make the final determination. We have all known people whose eternal destiny we questioned, and in some cases these people have left our lives without giving us an assurance of their "sonship."

But my hope is not deterred in the face of these uncertainties, for I have a confidence and an anticipation that God will one day reveal each and every one of His children. None will be missed; not one will be overlooked; no one will be forgotten. While I would desire every possible assurance that those I know will be with me in heaven, I also have the confident promise that one day all the sons—and daughters—of God will be revealed. He will not miss even one.

## Do the Math

We live in a brutal, unjust, corrupt world—a world of moral and spiritual pollution—a world that is dying, decaying, deadly, and dangerous. Without the hope that there is something more, that there is a day when the wrongs will be made right and the glory of God will be revealed, what do we have? If there is nothing beyond the wipers, just torrents of pain and the rain of suffering, why even keep moving? If this is all there is, then it just doesn't add up.

But God is already at work to restore the world and to redeem us. He is not away or asleep or unaware or unconcerned. No—He is at work. In fact, when we see the harsh realities of this world, we can be encouraged, for we know that all of the tragedy and the suffering will not equal all that will one day be revealed in, by, for, and to us.

## OUR HOPE PROVIDES
## FREEDOM FROM FUTILITY

The second rebar of hope that Romans 8 places in our hearts could be called the rebar of eternal purpose. This theme is laid throughout the remainder of this section of Romans 8. It is a centerpiece of our hope, providing us with a perspective that says, "There is a reason for our suffering; there is a purpose in our pain. Things may appear to be out of control, but our hope informs us that things are never out of God's plan."

As hard as it is to comprehend, there is something worse than pain, more difficult than affliction, more heartbreaking than suffering, and that is pain without purpose and hurt without hope.

### MEANINGLESSNESS IS HOPELESSNESS

Romans 8:20-21 underscores the pain of pointless suffering. As Paul speaks theologically in these verses, he implies that the fall of Adam resulted in one thing: Mankind was forced into a universe of meaninglessness. The curse pronounced on the creation following the fall of Adam is that of a loss of hope.

Following the Fall, the creation was "subjected to frustration," which is to say that as a result of mankind's separation from God, the world became shrouded in a cloak of ambiguity and confusion. We live in a fallen world, and we therefore struggle against meaninglessness, against life without lasting victory, against life with no clear purpose.

### THE FIRST CURSE

Consider the ultimate futility of even this most basic of tasks. Each season the field must be prepared. First, the ground has to be opened, for when left to itself, it closes up and grows hard. Then the seeds must be sown, seed after seed, row after row, acre after back-breaking acre.

Once the seeds are in place, you must battle the predators of the soil—the weeds and their allies. Even though you don't sow their seeds or cultivate them, they seem to grow faster and bigger and better than the plants you desire.

As your young plants begin to grow, the soil around them does not make itself more fertile and soft; instead, it closes in around your fragile seedlings and hardens so that you must constantly open it up and turn it over to keep it from choking out the tender life you are trying to protect. The insects that annoy you as you labor also feed on your young plants without your permission and usually without your benefit. Each day you must do battle with all these horticultural predators, for they attack without end and without discouragement.

Then, after months of risk and labor, when the harvest is finally ready, the produce requires immediate labor, or it will waste away and rot, for the crops do not do us the favor of harvesting themselves. And finally, most painful of all, the next season the entire cycle must be repeated all over again. Step by laborious step, season after season, year after year.

And for what?

So that we can live long enough so that we can get old enough to die.

Theologically speaking, the fall of Adam plunged mankind into a dark cycle of endless futility due to our separation from God. Without His presence, everything becomes meaningless. Without His guidance, life itself becomes only a pointless preparation for death. We were created to enjoy Him and to bring Him glory, and without this, life has no real purpose.

## THE POINT OF THE POINTLESSNESS

As my younger brother struggled through the days and nights of his injustice, he tasted the bitter fruit of suffering. His darkest hours came as he considered the senselessness of it all. His only hope was that God had a purpose in it. The only thing that allowed him to survive under the weight of his struggle was the steel of his hope that it was happening for a reason.

To suffer with no purpose is to suffer exponentially. To hurt with no hope makes the pain all the more intense. While we have not yet been delivered from the hurt and the pain and the struggle, we have been set free from the curse of futility.

All of the pain, all of the suffering, all of the injustices, and all of the struggles are working to produce a glorious result of God's design. We do not ever suffer in vain. We do not ever hurt without hope. We do not ever have pain without a purpose. We are set free for the glory of the sons of God.

## OUR HOPE MAKES SENSE OF
## OUR SUFFERING

The third rebar of hope in Romans 8:18-25 is placed parallel to the previous rebar, the rebar of eternal purpose. The repetition of this perspective strengthens our hope by reinforcing the truth that there is a purpose in our pain.

In Romans 8:22-23 the apostle Paul first places us in partnership with all of creation in our struggles. We are not alone in our suffering; all of creation is suffering with us. He then goes on to say that we do not struggle without a purpose. He compares our struggle and our suffering in this life to the struggle and suffering of a woman in labor: *"We know that the whole creation has been groaning as in the pains of childbirth right up to the present time. Not only so, but we ourselves, who have the firstfruits of the Spirit, groan inwardly as we wait eagerly for our adoption as sons, the redemption of our bodies."*

It is interesting to consider that the word for "groan" used here in verses 22 and 23 is the same word translated in Genesis 3:16 as "pain."[3] It is here in Genesis 3:16 that God pronounces additional curses as a result of the fall of Adam: *"To the woman he said, 'I will greatly increase your pains in childbearing; with pain you will give birth to children. Your desire will be for your husband, and he will rule over you.'"*

This is the groaning of anticipation. This is not to say that the pain is not genuine, but that there is a longing and an expectation mingled with the pain, similar to the pain of childbirth. Childbirth is the ultimate example of pain with a purpose. These are not the groans of hopelessness but the groans of impatience mingled with the pain.

## THE LESSONS OF LABOR

While I always hesitate to say this, knowing that there are any number of women for whom childbirth was a torturous experience, all of *our* children were delivered almost easily. But even this "ease" was not painless. We have no labor-room horror stories, no nightmare experiences with endless hours of labor, two or three shifts of nurses, or all-night delivery sessions.

Each of our three children was delivered naturally and relatively quickly. Our first daughter Cayah was almost born while we were filling out the paperwork in the hospital hallway. Our second daughter Leah came after much more time in the delivery room—and, as I recall, with significantly more pain.

With our third child Kaitlyn, the doctor was late. By the time he came into the delivery room and began putting on his gown and gloves, my lovely, patient wife was well past ready. She almost got up off the delivery table to strangle the doctor when he told her to hold on for a minute and not push because he had to put his shoe covers on.

While I am not able to repeat her exact words, suffice it to say that she felt very strongly that his ancestors and numerous others of his family members would suffer an extreme humiliation of their persons if he was not willing to immediately sacrifice one pair of shoes and deliver this baby. There was definitely some pain going on, and my wife was more than willing to share it if she did not get the cooperation she deserved.

### Been There but Not Done That

I have been fortunate enough to have played a part in the delivery of all three of my daughters. They do not call it "labor" for nothing. Each time I was in the delivery room, clothed in my dapper custom-made surgical green paper outfit, I was furiously wetting washcloths, providing ice chips, and coaching a variety of absurd breathing techniques. I like to tell everyone that "we" had a baby, but in truth "we" did no such thing.

There was only one person in those labor rooms who was "in labor." There was only one person in those delivery rooms who was actually "breathing" and "focusing" and "pushing." There was only one person lying on the delivery table giving birth, and it was not ever me or "we."

### Strictly Women's Work

You can be there all you want. You can attend a thousand deliveries. You can be the World Champion, all-star Lamaze Coach of the Century, but if you are a man, you will never ever "know" what it means to give birth to a child. Oh yeah, you may think you know. You may say you know. You may talk like you've been there and done that, but you will never "know." Even though Arnold Schwarzenegger may pretend to know what it means to be pregnant, remember why they call it "acting." No man will ever know what it is like to give birth. Forget it, pal; this is strictly woman's work.

### The Sense in the Suffering

Having said all this, I have one question: Why is there ever more than one child in any family? Realizing the pain and the trauma of childbirth, recognizing that there are no "we's" in the labor room, knowing that the experience of childbirth was capable of turning my mild-mannered, gentle-spirited wife into a gynecologically possessed, doctor-eating, in-your-face, birth-giving linebacker—why does any woman willingly repeat this process?

Many women deliver their children without the aid of drugs, so it cannot be that all women through the use of chemicals have forgotten the entire experience. Some people even videotape the birth of their children, so if they are tempted to romanticize the experience and forget what it was really like, they can replay the ordeal. The videotaped evidence should surely be a sufficient reminder, and yet even these women have more children.

Give a normal woman less than one year after the birth of her child and then go with her to the grocery store. Watch what happens. She will slow down her cart just to look longingly at the boxes of newborn Pampers, and then she will comment on how tiny and cute they are. She will linger over the cases of Similac and Enfamil. She may even brush her hands lovingly across the baby bottles and newborn infant clothes hanging on the racks.

Worst of all, however, is an encounter with another mother with an actual newborn in her arms. You would think that she just saw the Pope! She can become instantly hypnotized by this unknown newborn, as if she were powerless to ignore it. And the most amazing thing of all is that this fantasizing, cooing, and pursed-lips, kissy-baby talking takes place while her own child is there in the cart right in front of her.

"Oh, I'd love to have a baby," she might say to you, as you wonder what exactly that small gurgling creature is in the cart directly in front of her. "This one's too big to cuddle" is her logical response to your puzzled look.

Has she gone totally insane? Has she had some sort of infant-induced brain freeze? Has her selective memory completely blanked out the difficulties she herself went through in bringing a baby into the world? Is this some kind of psychotic state of denial?

No, it is none of these things. The obvious reason why any woman would willingly submit herself to the pain and the process of childbirth, ever, is because she understands the power of the product. The joy and the love that she has for her child so overpower the pain that it changes her perspective. It is a love so strong, a longing so powerful that not even the most painful experience of life can negate it.

## PREGNANT WITH HOPE

The love of a mother makes all of the pain worthwhile, and this is exactly the idea Jesus communicates to His disciples in John 16:20-22:

> I tell you the truth, you will weep and mourn while the world rejoices. You will grieve, but your grief will turn to joy. A woman giving birth to a child has pain because her time has come; but when her baby is born she forgets the anguish because of her joy that a child is born into the world. So with you: Now is your time of grief, but I will see you again and you will rejoice, and no one will take away your joy.

We may live in a violent and brutal and unfair and unjust and corrupt world. We will certainly face the pain of life as long as we live on this rebellious planet. But if the pain of our struggle is mixed with our longing for home, it is not purposeless pain. It is the pain of an expectant mother. It is not a senseless suffering; it is the ache of expectation mingled with the anticipation of eternity. Therefore, we do not struggle senselessly, but we suffer with the "labor pains" of life, empowered by the hope of heaven, anticipating the glorious delivery, looking to the birth of the promise that we will one day know a joy that no one can take away.

### Geological Groaning

According to verse 22, all of creation longs for this redemption. The entire creation is "in labor." Even as I write this, Hurricane Bertha is taking aim at the East Coast of the United States. Bertha is a relatively minor category-one hurricane, but don't tell that to the people whose homes and businesses are in its path. Its sea-churning winds have already ravaged the coastline from the Caribbean to New England. There are no "small" hurricanes when they are in your yard. Hurricane Bertha is a meteorological "groan." For it is just this power and fury that illustrate part of what I believe is the "groaning" of our planet.

As we see the earth rocked by volcanoes and earthquakes and hurricanes and typhoons and tornadoes, we can imagine that these are the "groans," the "labor pains" of creation. These are the geological and meteorological temper tantrums of a planet struggling to be at peace.

These are the labor pains of a planet awaiting its new birth. Each time we see the devastation these natural disasters cause, we can imagine that this is the creation groaning as it longs for the day of restoration.

Just as we might express our frustration in an isometric flex of our arms or in the clenching of our teeth and fists, so too nature grits its teeth and snaps its head in the frustration of longing. These expressions of frustration are the tremors of a planet trapped in anticipation of its own redemption. These "groanings" remind us of the hope we have, a hope even the creation reflects, and a redemption even the rocks anticipate.

### Appetizer Theology

My favorite restaurant in America is located here in Dallas. It is a wonderful place called Star Canyon, and it features a creative Southwestern cuisine. The most famous item on their unusual menu is a specially prepared rib eye steak. Anyone who goes to Star Canyon should be required by law to eat it at least once. Yet this is not the most unique feature of this wonderful restaurant. For at Star Canyon, each menu features a full page of delightfully exotic appetizers—a full 50 percent of the menu.

One of the first times I went there, I had a marvelous shrimp fajita appetizer unlike anything I had ever tasted in my life. I discovered taste buds that I did not even know I had. I could not believe that anyone could make something so odd-sounding taste so good.

When our waiter returned to inquire how our appetizers were, I informed him that I would not be needing anything else for the rest of the meal. The shrimp fajita had done me in. I was not planning to brush my teeth for the next week so that the flavor of that marvelous appetizer might linger in my mouth.

After the waiter had politely finished with his professional chuckling,[4] he said, "If you thought that was good, just wait for the rib eye." My eyes lit up like a child who had just seen his name on the biggest present under the Christmas tree. How could anything be better? Was he serious, or was that just waiter-speak? My anticipation was on overload as I waited for the tantalizing rib eye.

Consider the implications: If this rib eye steak was better than what I had already tasted, it would be the best thing I had ever eaten in my life. My taste buds were warmed up and limber, preparing to do a routine like an Olympic gymnast. The hair on the back of my neck was standing on end. Every time a waiter appeared with a tray of food on his shoulder, I salivated. The sound of kitchen doors opening created a Pavlovian response within my glands. John Philip Sousa might have been at my elbow, lifting his baton for a great march. I had tasted the heavenly appetizer, and now I was groaning with each passing moment, waiting for the arrival of the heavenly main course.

It came. I tasted. And I discovered that the rib eye was *that* good. Just thinking about it makes me hungry. But I have not forgotten the lesson of the appetizer. On its own, it was amazing. It was a meal all by itself. But it was not the main course; it was simply the foretaste. If I thought the appetizer was great, the rest of the meal was even more spectacular.

## The Taste of Heaven

In some way this is why the suffering makes sense—because this life is not the entree. Being satisfied with the appetizer makes as much sense as being satisfied with just being pregnant. Part of our struggle is that we know this is not all there is. We have tasted heaven, and yet we ache for more. If even the creation groans for a day of redemption, then should we expect any less discomfort? This life was never meant to "fill us up"; it is only created to prepare us for the "main course."

We live in a world of moral and spiritual pollution, and we long for the clear air of heaven. But this longing is not pointless, for we anticipate, along with all of creation, a place and a time when we will no longer struggle but will receive our full adoption as children.

All of our suffering is mingled with our dissatisfaction in this life and anticipation of heaven. We should not be surprised at our struggle, for we not only live in a fallen and mutinous world, but we have already received the firstfruits of our deliverance. Of course we ache! We are groaning for the entree, for the delivery, for the fulfillment of heaven.

## OUR HOPE MAKES THE WAIT
## WORTHWHILE

The final rebar of hope in Romans 8:18-25 crisscrosses the first three. Our hope is reinforced once again by the reminder in verses 24 and 25 of our eternal perspective and eternal purpose: *"For in this hope we were saved. But hope that is seen is no hope at all. Who hopes for what he already has? But if we hope for what we do not yet have, we wait for it patiently."*

Woven within these two small verses is a tapestry that portrays the character of hope in a way that defies their compact size. The word *hope* appears more times—five—in these two verses than it does in some other chapters or even entire books of the Bible.[5]

### THE HOPE THAT SAVES

As my brother struggled through the seemingly endless weeks following the false accusations of his misconduct, it was his hope that saved him. His hope of justice, his hope of acquittal, and his hope of heaven all sustained him. It was his hope that allowed him to press on, not to give up, and to continue to do good.

The mother in the delivery room, the recruit in boot camp, and the student in medical school can survive the ordeal because of their hope. The hope of birth, promotion, and graduation save them from collapsing under the load. There is an end worth waiting for. There is a prize worth running for. There is a victory worth fighting for. This is the nature of hope. And this is how hope saves us.

### Life Is Just Waiting

Rebecca was one of the most beautiful young women I have ever known. She had the kind of beauty that transcended her attractive appearance. Her beauty radiated from her heart. She was intelligent, intensely spiritual, extremely talented, and unwavering in her pursuit of excellence. Having known her since before she was in junior high school, my wife and I were aware that her entire life was characterized by this beauty. She was the pride and joy of her parents and a prized friend of all who knew her.

Her beauty was taken from us this past Wednesday. In one of those tragic events that plague our mutinous planet, her life ended in an unrepeatable instant. Without warning, without explanation, without anticipation, as she walked along a familiar road, she inadvertently stepped out in front of an oncoming automobile, and before she could have realized her mistake, she was gone.

Even though she died in a moment, it took almost ten hours for her family to receive the news. Once again I found myself seated among the small congregations of grief, completely exhausted, empty of any satisfactory explanations, left alone to rely on the power of hope and the silence of a tearful embrace for comfort.

As family and friends gathered in that all-too-familiar context of sorrow, Rebecca's father and I went into a side room to talk and make arrangements for the days ahead. We spoke to people from all over the country—some who knew this beautiful young woman and some who simply knew of her. Her father's resolve in the face of this tragedy was overwhelming. The depth of his pain and the significance of his loss were as great as any we can know.

After one of the phone calls, he quietly hung up, turned to me, and said, "I guess that's the point, Dave."

"Excuse me?" I imagined I had missed the first part of his statement.

"The point of this kind of thing. The point of heaven," he said.

My puzzled look urged him to continue. "Heaven. That's the point—heaven. More than ever, that is where I want to be—where I can see her again and talk to her again and . . . hold her again."

He paused as if momentarily transported to that place and that day. Then he finished, "Now the rest of my life will just be waiting."

As his lip trembled and his eyes pressed closed, I got the point.

## The Light of Heaven

In the pitch blackness of the greatest tragedy a parent could ever face, only the hope of heaven can shine in. The years will pass, and the tears will flow, and while healing will take place, the grieving will never really end. Rebecca's parents will always think of her and miss her. Birthdays, holidays, anniversaries of special events will always, and should always, rekindle memories and, along with them, the lingering burn of grief and "what might have been." No one ever "gets over" a loss like this, not in this lifetime. I will miss her for the rest of mine.

But what sustains us through this unending wilderness and guides us through this darkness is the hope of heaven—the hope that one day we will see her again, that one day we will embrace her and never have to let her go again.

There will be a time when the days of struggle and separation will be erased by an eternity without good-byes. There will be a place where the burden of pain and grief will be obliterated by a joy that overwhelms into nonexistence all that once had been. This is how our hope saves us.

## THE CHRISTMAS EVE PRINCIPLE

In one final stroke, Paul places the last reinforcement within our hope, and it is perhaps the most puzzling. It is the rebar of patience.

Where does this patience come from?

Why on earth must we wait patiently for the time when our hope will become sight?

What is the value of patience in the midst of the pain?

Waiting is hard, and it is made harder still by the painless glory of what we are waiting for. How are we to be patient when what we await is the most desirable thing we could ever imagine?

When it is the goal and the focus of our faith, how and why should we wait for it patiently?

I suppose that most middle class Americans of the Baby Boomer generation share my memories of Christmas, or more precisely, the memories of the hours before Christmas morning. These were some of the longest hours in my life. During the time of anticipation before the gift-giving orgy on Christmas morning, each minute seemed a lifetime. Even though I was exiled to my bedroom for the final hours before sunrise, sleep was impossible. In all of my childhood experience, I never knew such anticipation. Patience was not a virtue to me during these hours; it was a curse.

To this day I retain vivid memories of my sister's and my descent in the predawn hours to survey the marvelous array of gifts piled at the foot of the sparkling Christmas tree. On more than one occasion my parents awoke, found the hour to be too early, and physically forced us back to our rooms. One particular year they actually had to lash my door closed in order to prevent my continued quarterly hour arousal of our entire family.

Isn't this the attitude we should have toward heaven?

If the glory of eternity, the presence of Christ, and the reunion of the saints are not our most anticipated moments, then what are?

Is not our discomfort with the wait an expression of our longing and our hope?

Shouldn't we be scratching and clawing at the gates of heaven, anxious for them to open?

How can Paul say that in light of this hope we wait for it "patiently"?

## A PROFESSIONAL HOPE

Over the years I have had the privilege to get to know a number of professional athletes—men who make their living in competition, regularly anticipating a contest, staring into the face of great reward. These men are involved in a variety of professional sports, from football to golf, from basketball to auto racing. Some of these men have been and are the very best in the world at what they do. At the least, they have achieved a level of success that most normal people like me can only dream of. I have watched them on a number of occasions as they anticipated a playoff game, a championship round, or a big race, and they all shared one unusual trait—patience.

Most of us, as we anticipate a major event or contest, behave like a kid before Christmas morning. We are nervous, anxious, pacing about like caged animals. This is probably why we are not world champions at anything. The professionals I know respond quite the opposite. They show incredible self-control and patience. Their concentration transforms their anticipation into a serenity that empowers them in the upcoming contest.

The most vivid illustration I have ever seen of this pre-contest patience came as I visited a world-champion race driver. He is not only one of the best drivers alive, but he is perhaps one of the best ever. He certainly looks forward to the time he spends racing; in fact, for him, it is only when he is in his race car that he is most fully alive. Even though he has been racing most of his life and has won just about everything he could possibly win, he still hates to lose. He lives to race and races to win.

Yet I know that in the hours before a big race, you will often find him in his motor coach or in the suite of his race trailer sound asleep. Doctors who have monitored his blood pressure and heart rate before, during, and after a race have found that just prior to a race, his heart rate is actually *slower* than normal.

His patience is certainly not rooted in complacency or disinterest. His patience and the patience of other professionals like him is founded upon one thing—his unwavering confidence in his ability to win. Too often we think that patience is related to apathy or a lack of excitement, enthusiasm, or commitment, when genuine patience is actually built upon an unshakable confidence.

## A PATIENT HOPE

Waiting is hard, especially when we consider the significance of what we are waiting for. The more we anticipate, the harder the wait. The more desperately we want to be somewhere, the more irrelevant our present surroundings seem. But if we are supremely confident of our arrival, if we have no doubt about our victory, if our reunion with those we love is sure, then in waiting we have no anxiety, no apprehension, and no need to hurry. The Bible never records that Jesus ever ran anywhere, and He was never late, even to Calvary.

Patience is a mark of confidence, a sign of assurance, and an indication of maturity for the believer. When we endure trials patiently, we communicate to those around us our confidence in our hope. While we may long for the restoration of our relationships and the redemption of our lives, while we do cry out, "Maranatha! Come quickly, Lord Jesus," we can stand up under the trials and wait for heaven patiently because we are certain of it.

## THE FRUIT OF HOPE

Fortunately the trauma that engulfed my brother's life did not destroy his ministry entirely. During the months of investigation, interview, and interrogation, he was wisely allowed to continue most of his regular duties. He never communicated his anguish to most of those he came in contact with. He pressed on and continued "to do good."

In his perseverance he was demonstrating the patient confidence of a professional. When we spoke on the phone, he expressed his inner longing for resolution. He ached and groaned for redemption. His desire for heaven was never more acute. During all this time, the reality of the pain never went away. Yet all those he encountered and all those he served in ministry saw only the fruit of his hope—his patient service. His hope saw him through.

At the close of the season, before the charges had been officially determined to be false, Peter's boss called him into his office. Even though by that time it looked as though Peter would be cleared, Peter had lived the past months under close investigative scrutiny and endured daily heartache, and his boss knew it.

As he invited my brother to take a seat, he pointed to a stack of papers on his office desk. These were evaluation forms filled out by people who had been involved in Peter's ministry over the past few months. These people did not simply make note of mere facts regarding Peter's service; one after another, they mentioned very specifically Peter's attitude during this time.

In his boss's office, Peter sat wide-eyed, listening as his boss read comment after comment describing the "Christlikeness," the "Christlike attitude," and the "godliness" people had seen in working with my brother. None of these people had any idea what he was facing. None of these evaluations had been specifically designed to elicit comments about Peter or his role in the ministry. Yet on page after page his name appeared, and along with it came the unanimous affirmation of godly behavior. The voice of the Lord Himself was in those comments. It was the voice of vindication and commendation for a job well done.

It was the voice of hope.

# EIGHT

# The Prayer of Hope

*In the same way,*
*the Spirit helps us in our weakness.*
*We do not know what we ought to pray for,*
*but the Spirit himself intercedes for us*
*with groans that words cannot express.*
*And he who searches our hearts*
*knows the mind of the Spirit,*
*because the Spirit intercedes for the saints*
*in accordance with God's will.*

*Romans 8:26-27*

The military calls it a PRC-112—"Personal Radio Communicator 112." A PRC-112 is a five-by-two-inch, mostly plastic, twenty-eight-ounce, high-tech walkie-talkie. Compared to the sophisticated electronics and avionics equipment carried on a twenty-million-dollar F-16, this plastic radio seems almost toylike. However, in life-or-death situations, it is no toy; it is a priceless piece of equipment.

## ONE BAD DAY

On Friday afternoon, June 2, 1995, Air Force Captain Bob "Wilbur" Wright and his wing man, Air Force Captain Scott "Zulu" O'Grady, were on a mission over northern Serb-controlled Bosnia, just south of the town of Banja Luka. Their mission in support of "Operation Deny Flight" was designed to take them near but not directly over known

Serbian antiaircraft missile sites. As their mission proceeded into the late afternoon of June 2, the two pilots had no idea that during the previous night the Serbian forces had relocated their SA-6 antiaircraft missiles directly beneath their flight path.

At exactly 3:03 in the afternoon the radar warning receiver in Captain O'Grady's F-16 indicated that he was being targeted by a missile. In fighter-pilot speak, he was "spiked."

> Nine seconds after the spike, I saw a brilliant red flash to my right; a missile had exploded between my plane and Wilbur's.
>     We weren't safe yet. SA-6s come packaged in racks of three. Sure enough, Wilbur screamed: "Missiles in the air!"
>     But I never heard Wilbur. Within a second after that red flash, all I could hear was the murderous bang that swallowed me whole, like the whale that got Jonah. All I could feel was the biggest jolt of my life. I knew a little something about crashes, but this one took first prize. It was like getting rear-ended by a speeding eighteen-wheeler with an explosive warhead strapped to its hood.
>     When a plane and missile collide, the plane finishes second.[1]

The SA-6 missile hit the underside of O'Grady's F-16, cutting the jet in two. At the time of impact he had been flying at 26,000 feet and well over 500 miles per hour. In the fraction of a second following the impact, O'Grady miraculously managed to eject from his disintegrating aircraft, which disappeared instantly into the clouds below. The explosion and thick cloud deck beneath Captain Wright did not allow him to see if his wing man had escaped his exploding aircraft. The last image he carried back from Bosnia that day was that of a horrific fireball and the unknown fate of his comrade.

For the next six days Captain Scott O'Grady hid in the perilous Bosnian countryside. He camouflaged himself and lay motionless for hours at a time. He moved only in the darkness of night and constantly lived within a few steps of discovery and capture. He survived by eating bugs, grass, and leaves, and by drinking water wrung from his filthy socks.

Even as all of the technical abilities and concentrated skills of the entire Western military alliance attempted to locate and rescue Captain O'Grady, his most important single possession turned out to be his toylike PRC-112. This pocket radio was his only means of communication with the military power waiting to rescue him. As it turned out, his best source of hope was perhaps the simplest and least sophisticated piece of electronic equipment in the entire military.

## FOXHOLE THEOLOGIANS

Being shot down behind enemy lines can provide a person with a whole new view of life. Hiding in unknown enemy territory can cause a person to cling to whatever hope is available, no matter how simple. It is perhaps an indictment of our own apathy that we realize the truth of this only after we're shot down behind enemy lines, wounded, and fighting for our survival (metaphorically speaking). We are, at best, foxhole theologians and POW prayer warriors.

This may sound harsh, but most of us treat prayer as if it were a cheap child's toy. When we are not taking it for granted, we are ignoring it entirely. In our difficult and confusing lives, we tend to rely on more "sophisticated" or "high-tech" sources of hope. Prayer seems too simple, too easy, perhaps even too weak. When the crises of life can destroy a home and wipe out a lifetime of work, prayer appears too small a remedy.

Do you know what it is like to live uncertain of your future—to live moment by moment and day to day, feeling as if your next moment may bring chaos and disaster?

Have you ever lost hope as you battled the conflicts of life?

Do you grow weary from the fight?

Do all of your plans and resources for finding freedom seem unreliable and ineffective?

Have you given up on prayer?

Or have you sought to find hope in the simplest of God's gifts, the gift of communication with Him?

I can assure you, you are not alone in your struggle, and you are not alone in your doubts, for prayer is far more powerful than most of us realize.

### The Power of Prayer

Because prayer is simple and uncomplicated does not mean that it is not powerful. In fact, its simplicity indicates its true power. You see, even the simplest prayer easily reaches God's ear. The sincere cry of a hurting heart always finds God's care. There is no sophistication or eloquence required for anyone, from any tongue, from anyplace, at anytime, to enter into God's presence. No reservations required. You don't need to call ahead. The simplest cry of a broken heart can work to secure eternal life. Do not be misled by the childlike simplicity of prayer; its simplicity is its power and our powerful hope.

Romans 8:26-27 gives us a behind-the-scenes look at what happens when we pray. The sophistication and power of prayer show up well out of our view, and these verses reveal the activity we cannot see. The most uncomplicated plea stirs into action a most mysterious and powerful course of events. Just as Captain O'Grady could only imagine the powerful forces awaiting his communication, so too we can only imagine the might of God poised in anticipation of our call.

### THE MARVELOUS PROMISE OF PRAYER: THE SPIRIT INTERCEDES

*In the same way, the Spirit helps us in our weakness. We do not know what we ought to pray for, but the Spirit himself intercedes for us with groans that words cannot express.*

To discover the real promise of prayer, we must first *admit we don't know how to pray.* This is not due to a lack of information. Prayer seminars, sermons, meetings, and retreats fill our calendars; books and videos about prayer fill the shelves of our homes and bookstores. We do not know how to pray because of our lack of comprehension.

We begin to know the promise of prayer when we accept our limitations.

How can we assume to know the best possible course for the

future? How can we claim to know all the complex details of the perfect plan of God?

We can barely comprehend our own hearts and motives; how then are we to pray for the needs and desires hidden in the hearts of others?

When we understand that our impure motives and limited perspectives cloud our view, then we can begin to understand the marvelous promise of prayer.

These limitations ought not to discourage our prayer, but rather empower it. You see, the promise of Romans 8:26 is that the Spirit intercedes when we do not know how we should pray. He knows what we do not. He understands what we cannot. He has full information and complete comprehension. He has the mind of God to know the hearts of men. This is our hope. Our prayer need not be perfect, for He perfects it.

## THE HOLY SPIRIT COMPREHENDS
## OUR NEEDS PERFECTLY

We may not know exactly how to pray, but the Spirit does. When we pray, the promise is that the Spirit makes up for our inadequacies. The phrase "helps us in our weakness" provides us with an illuminating word picture of the role of the Holy Spirit in prayer. The phrase is actually just one word in Greek συναντιλαμβάνω (*sunantilambano*). This is a compound word—a root word with two prefixes. The first prefix συν (*sun*) means "with." The second prefix is αντι (*anti*) which, as you might guess, means "against." And the root word is λαμβανω (lambano), which can mean "to walk" or "to carry." In normal usage the word meant "to share with" or "to come to the aid of." But in a literal sense it means "to walk or carry against."

The literal image conveyed by the phrase "helps us in our weakness" is that of a heavy load that must be carried by two persons—a large stone or a heavy trunk that two people would have to grasp on either end and carry together while facing each other.

This is the precise image of Romans 8:26. The Holy Spirit carries the other end of the load. He shares the burden with us. This first means that we have a responsibility; we have an end to carry. It is important to notice that Romans 8:26 implies that the Spirit's help begins *when* we pray. We have to make the call. We have to turn on the transmitter and make contact. The Holy Spirit does not pray *instead* of us or when we will not, but he "helps" us when we do pray. He prays along with us. The promise of Romans 8:26 is that when we lift up our burdens, He will share the load.

Second, this promise reminds us that the Spirit is personally aware of the weight of our burden. If He is lifting it along with us, then He is well aware of the load. Because we don't know how to pray does not mean that we should not pray; in fact, the opposite is true. For it is when we grab hold of our burdens, those that we cannot lift alone, that we apprehend the marvelous promise that the Holy Spirit will not leave us to struggle by ourselves. He fully and perfectly comprehends the weight we bear, for He lifts it with us.

## THE HOLY SPIRIT COMMUNICATES OUR NEEDS PERFECTLY

The phrase *"but the Spirit himself intercedes for us with groans that words cannot express"* have been the focus of constant discussion and a wide variety of interpretations. All this theological rabble-rousing has been over the question, most simply put: Exactly what is the nature of these "groans" or "utterances" that the Spirit makes on our behalf? Is this an indication of a "Spirit language" or a "heavenly tongue"? Are these words inaudible or inexpressible or both? This discussion has seemed to divide as many believers as it has confused interpreters.

### The Groaning Spirit

At this point I am confident that no one can say for sure exactly how the Holy Spirit communicates. Our best guesses and personal opinions will have to do for now. However, I find great hope in the realization that the Holy Spirit has some abilities that I do not. Even though I am empowered by Him, He still has abilities that I cannot possess. He is God. I ought never to think that I can fully comprehend or perfectly imitate Him, for then He would be no greater than I. One of these unique supernatural abilities is His capacity for communication, these "groanings" that are more perfect and more powerful than any I might produce.

COMPRESSION COMPREHENSION. In our computer-savvy world

the terms *encryption* and *compression* are familiar to most of us. Encryption is a technical term for the encoding of messages. Many people understand Romans 8:27 to teach that the Holy Spirit is encrypting our prayers. In other words, "groans" implies that He puts our prayers into a kind of heavenly code that only God Himself can unscramble. Our hope then comes from the idea that we too can speak in this code and join with the Spirit in our intercession.

On the other hand, compression technology allows a computer user to take large amounts of data and store them or transfer them in a much smaller space. This could be called "macro-data." However, the sense of compression I am using here is far less technical and somewhat more personal. For we typically use forms of compression in our personal communication every day. While we may not realize it, we compress data all the time.

LOVE GRUNTS. When my children scream, they are using compression technology. If their scream is an ear-piercing, monosyllabic, sirenlike cry, it can mean either they have encountered some life-threatening pain, and I must come to their aid immediately, or more likely they are fighting with their sisters over some article of clothing. If their scream is a modified high-pitched giggle, it usually indicates that they have just found out something of great social or personal value, probably involving a telephone and a boy. My familiarity with their lives allows me to gather a great deal of data from one simple scream. It is my job; I am a father.

My wife too is able to compress her communication simply by using the tone of her voice when she says something as common as the word *dear*. On the one hand, with this one utterance (often used to identify small woodland creatures with little white tails and names like Bambi) I can understand that I have once again failed in my spousal responsibilities by leaving my socks in an undesignated space.

If the tone of her voice is low, kind of like a growling bear, I know right away that my labor as a loving husband is being called into question, probably because I put something in the dishwasher without washing it first (duh) or I dried an article of clothing which, due to its mysterious fabric content, has been turned into Barbie clothes by the heat of our dryer.

On the other hand, when the tone of her voice sounds more like a person communicating with an infant and sometimes includes the appendages "Oh" or "My sweet," it can mean she is empathetically seeking to bring me comfort and love or possibly preparing to ask for money. I know what these things mean. It is my job; I am a husband.

At the end of a day, almost any husband and wife can use compression technology to communicate how their day went simply through connected sighs, groans, grunts, and harumphs. No real words need be spoken. Each sound carries a meaning far beyond its etymological value because of the relationship between the two parties. Each inflection carries great meaning, even though to the casual observer this communication may appear almost meaningless, certainly indecipherable, even somewhat apelike. It may not sound too romantic, but in some cases, a good "haaarumph" can be the language of love.

### Pregnant with Meaning

When we are in a close relationship with someone, compression takes place in much of our communication. Sighs, screams, laughs, and single words become pregnant with meaning. They are "dense" in their data, packed with information. This information is fully understood by the recipient due to the intimacy with the sender. I like to believe that this type of compression takes place as the Holy Spirit, who knows both our hearts and the heart of God, sighs and groans with great passion and inflection in His communication on our behalf.

No words can fully express these compressed communications because they are both indications of and expressions of an intimate relationship. It is in this perfect communication that we can find great hope. We can find hope in the promise that the Holy Spirit not only knows the depths of our hearts, but that He also is perfectly and powerfully interceding on our behalf.

### Perfect Personal Communication

For all of this fascinating theological and technical speculation, the one thing we know without a doubt and upon which all believers can agree is that the Spirit is *personally* involved in our intercession.

Regardless of how one understands the nuances of these "groanings," they serve as a powerful reminder of the Holy Spirit's personal involvement in our lives. He Himself communicates for us. No matter how we might prefer to understand the nature of His communication, the Spirit's intercession gives us confidence and hope—we never pray in vain, and we never pray alone.

The marvelous promise of prayer is that we are never alone, never abandoned, and never unheard, even in our simplest and least eloquent cry to God. The Holy Spirit perfectly comprehends our burdens as He carries them with us. The Holy Spirit also perfectly communicates our concerns in ways that we cannot begin to comprehend.

When you are wondering whether anyone is listening, when you are doubting whether anything you say makes it past the ceiling, when words fail you and you do not even know what to say, remember the promise of Romans 8:26 and have hope.

## THE MYSTERIOUS POWER OF PRAYER: THE TRINITY INTERACTS

In the early morning hours of Thursday, June 8, 1995, Captain Thomas Oren "T. O." Hanford and his wing man Clark Highstrete were completing their surveillance mission just off the eastern coast of Bosnia. With an additional forty minutes of fuel on board, Captain Hanford requested permission to remain in the air over Bosnia to help in the search for the American pilot shot down six days before, Captain Scott O'Grady. With permission, Hanford stayed on watch, searching and listening in the night sky for any sign of his downed comrade. He flew with his powerful radio turned to its most sensitive settings, listening through the storm of static and calling out into the night, "Basher Five-Two, this is Basher One-One on Alpha." Nothing but the constant shower of static filled his headphones for close to forty minutes.

At 2:06 A.M., while pointing toward Bosnia on his hot leg, Hanford recited his call for the umpteenth time. He felt dispirited, as though he were just going through the motions. In a few minutes he'd have to give the search up.

Then he heard something behind the wall of static, so faint that he might have imagined it: *"Basher One-One . . . Basher Five-Two."* The voice sounded feeble, lethargic, but Hanford wasn't jumping to conclusions. . . .

"This is Basher One-One," Hanford said, enunciating with extra care. "I can barely hear you—say your call sign."

Once again he did hear it: *"Basher One-One . . . Basher Five-Two."* . . .

Hanford was still unsure. "Understand that you are Basher Five-Two. This is Basher One-One on Alpha."

And then he heard it, really heard it, still weak and parched-sounding, but now familiar and definitely there: *"This is Basher Five-Two. Read you loud and clear. . . . I'm alive, I'm alive!"*

"Copy that!" Hanford said. He could feel the tears forming. Though he knew who it was, Hanford needed some authentication to get the rescue ball rolling and to ensure that no one would be heading into a Bosnian Serb ambush. He needed to ask for something no outsider would know—some fact I would never reveal in captivity. Hanford had served at Kunsan Air Base with the Pantons, and he knew my history there.

"What was your squadron in Korea?" Hanford said.

*"Juvats—Juvats!"*

"Copy that, you're alive! Good to hear your voice!" This was less than standard radio discipline, but Hanford was literally shaking with emotion. He struggled to regain some control; it was hard to fly an F-16 with tears streaming down your face.[2]

## THE AFFIRMATION OF THE INVISIBLE

With Captain Hanford's confirmation of Scott O'Grady's survival and location, the entire American military machine went into action. As Captain O'Grady impatiently crouched, alone and cold, on a hilltop in the middle of enemy territory, hundreds of men and women were rushing to his aid. Even though he could not see them, even though he did not know their names, they knew him, and they were on their way.

Within half an hour of Captain O'Grady's first communication, the commander of all of NATO's southern forces, four-star Admiral Leighton "Snuffy" Smith, was preparing the orders for Captain

O'Grady's rescue, even though the admiral's offices were thousands of miles away in London.

Shortly before 3:00 A.M., Admiral Smith contacted Marine Colonel Martin Berndt, who was stationed off the coast of Bosnia on board the helicopter carrier *Kearsarge*. Within the hour Colonel Berndt woke up his young marines. Shortly before 3:30 A.M. (9:30 P.M. Washington time) the President of the United States had heard of O'Grady's radio broadcast. By 4:39 A.M., less than two and a half hours after Scott O'Grady's first contact with Captain Hanford, Colonel Berndt's elite Search and Rescue team of forty-one marines boarded helicopters to head for Bosnia.

## THE ACCOMPLISHMENT OF THE IMPOSSIBLE

All of this action began through the power of a twenty-eight-ounce, handheld, battery-powered, toylike walkie-talkie. The PRC-112 Scott O'Grady used as he hid in the Bosnian forests had a very limited broadcast range. On a clear night from an unobstructed hilltop, the signal might travel 100 miles. This is a faint blip compared to the high-powered transmission devices in the aircraft flying over his head. But when his little transmitter made contact with one of the powerful receivers above him, he was heard halfway around the world.

His message was carried all the way to the corridors of power at the Pentagon and the White House half a world away in Washington, D.C. In the same way, our words alone do not have the power to reach the corridors of heaven; it is the Spirit who has the power. The Holy Spirit speaks with an amplification that our tiny voices could never achieve.

Romans 8:27 gives us a behind-the-scenes look at the amplification and activity that take place when we pray. As Captain O'Grady huddled in hiding under the cold, clear Bosnian night sky, he had only the hope that his communication would bring about his rescue. He had to cling to this hope alone without seeing all the activity his communication had instigated.

Our hope is like that. It is a hope that when we find ourselves struggling to survive and crying out for help, our communication has initiated a supernatural response. Romans 8:27 reveals what we are unable to see as we pray—the supernatural power that our communication has unleashed.

## THE ATTENTION OF THE IMMORTAL

Just how powerful is prayer?

When we pray, heaven listens. When we pray, the Creator of the universe pays attention. The foundations of heaven shake, and the forces of God move. When we pray, the resources that formed the universe are placed on alert, and the Father, the Son, and the Holy Spirit all get involved.

### The Trinitarian Schematic

If you are paying attention theologically, you may notice that Romans 8:27 may be a Trinitarian schematic—a technical and theological map of the power source of prayer: *"And he who searches our hearts knows the mind of the Spirit, because the Spirit intercedes for the saints in accordance with God's will."*

HE SEARCHES OUR HEARTS. Who is the "he" who searches our hearts? Many interpreters—in fact, most interpreters—believe this person to be the Spirit. He is the object of this passage and the subject of these verses. However, why then is "he" also the one who "knows the mind of the Spirit" if they are the same person? The "he" at the beginning of verse 27 could be understood to be the Son, Jesus Christ. He is the one who searches our hearts and who knows the mind of the Spirit.

While the Scriptures depict the Father, the Son, and the Spirit each knowing and searching men's hearts, consider the ability to know what was in the hearts of men that Christ demonstrated. We have sufficient reason to believe that Jesus not only knows the hearts of men, but that He also has this ability among the Trinity.

THE MIND OF THE SPIRIT. With this schematic in mind, we believe that Jesus Christ is the "he" who knows the mind of the Spirit. To know the mind of the Spirit in this context implies that Jesus can understand and interpret the "groans" that the Spirit is communicating on behalf of "the saints" (us).

THE WILL OF THE FATHER. This communication is guided and shaped according to the will of God—that is to say, the Father. In this schematic, the Son, the Spirit, and the Father are each intimately involved in the activity of prayer.

All of this mysterious inter-Trinitarian communication may be impossible and even unnecessary for us to fully understand. But even in our most basic understanding of this passage, we can know that God is fully and completely involved when we pray. We have His full attention. Every aspect of the Trinity has a part in prayer.

Prayer is not some cursory religious function that simply contributes to our piety. It is not just a ritualistic discipline without purpose. According to the message of Romans 8:27, prayer cannot be seen as a secondary activity in heaven. Prayer involves the same focus and power as the creation of the world; it involves all of who God is—Father, Son, and Holy Spirit.

### The Power of Unity

Why does Paul bother to tell us all of this technical and theological information about the Trinity? We cannot possibly understand it. He does not give enough information for us to have a full picture of the activity in heaven when we pray; he simply cracks the door open to let us peek in. Why tell us only this and no more? How does this implication of unity between the Father, Son, and Holy Spirit help us? In one word: Hope.

This behind-the-scenes glimpse into the activity in heaven is designed to increase our conviction, our confidence, and our passion when we pray. Just knowing that God knows our needs intimately should be enough to increase our conviction about prayer. This flash of information, this theological sound bite, should be enough to give us hope that there is great power and promise in our prayer. God is one with us and for us. To know this is sufficient cause for us to run eagerly into His presence. Or is it?

### THE CONVICTION OF OUR CONVICTIONS

The question is not why should we pray, but why don't we? (*If this is too convicting, you may want to skip ahead to the next chapter.*) If we are honest, most of us will admit that we don't pray as we should. Even the greatest prayer warrior understands the limits and frailty of his prayer life. Most believers spend only a few minutes a week in prayer. Statistics show that the average *pastor* only spends *fifteen minutes a week* in prayer, and I am convinced that this estimate is optimistic.

Why, in light of the power and promise of prayer, do we struggle to develop any real consistency in prayer?

I am sure there are many reasons. We are too busy; we are stuck on the treadmill of life, and it is set to uphill-fast. Perhaps we are simply too self-reliant. We are taught from a young age to look out for number one—not God, but us. Perhaps a few of us are uncertain how to pray. There may be a handful of sincere believers who simply don't know enough about prayer to be motivated to pray more consistently and passionately.

### Unbelieving Believers

However, for all of our excuses, I believe we don't pray simply because we don't believe in it. We look at the weak little transmitter we call prayer and wonder how it can be heard outside of our room. Once again, prayer seems too simple, too childlike, too weak. We are not sure prayer works; we doubt that it really matters. We grow skeptical and doubtful as our prayers seem to produce unpredictable answers. We demand better results. Is it any wonder then that we struggle to maintain hope when we so readily discard this powerful tool?

This may be too critical, but I know from my own experience that I don't pray as I should. I really don't pray as though I believe in the power and promise of prayer, for if I did, you could not keep me from doing it. If we fully realized just a little bit of the power in Romans 8:26-27, how could we not pray? We would seize every opportunity to run to the presence of God.

### The Mark of a Hero

Each evening for six days, Captain Scott O'Grady turned on his PRC-112 as he hid in the forests of Bosnia. For six days he heard no answer. For six days he didn't know if anyone heard his transmissions. He had no way of knowing if his radio was even working correctly. But each night he called out, and night after night he waited.

Can you imagine what would have happened if Scott O'Grady had discarded his radio? Imagine that he decided it was no use to continue to waste his time calling out on this silly plastic toy, and in frustration and anger tossed his radio aside. What would we think of a young pilot who simply limited his transmissions to a few times a week, perhaps just before he ate a meal of leaves and bugs or just before he lay down to sleep?

What if his transmissions were limited to once or twice a week, simply a sentence or two he shot off on a Sunday morning? How different would this story be if, after six days without a response, a frustrated young fugitive stuffed his radio into his vest and gave up an hour before Captain Hanford turned on his receiver?

Scott O'Grady was a hero because he never gave up. He believed that he had a powerful, loyal, and mighty ally searching for even his faintest transmission. Even though for six days he heard nothing other than static from his little plastic hand-held radio, he never stopped believing in it. He knew of the commitment of his comrades, and he knew that his childlike radio was all he needed to get through to them. In the early morning of Thursday, June 8, when he heard Captain T. O. Hanford respond, "Good to hear your voice," he had all the confirmation he needed.

### Send in the Cavalry

The "package" of aircraft and marines assembled in the early hours just before dawn, eighty-seven miles west of Scott O'Grady's position, was the largest put together since the Gulf War. It included Cobra helicopter gunships, CH-53 Super Stallions, F-16 and F-15 fighters, tank-killing A-10 Warthogs, F/A-18 Hornets, EF-111 Aardvarks, Marine Corps Harrier Jump-jets, and EA-6 Prowlers. Along with this armada of aircraft, there were eight flying tankers and a second team of identical helicopters and aircraft waiting on standby in case something went wrong with the first team.

Shortly after 6:35 A.M. on Thursday, June 8, the cavalry arrived. The pastoral Bosnian countryside was suddenly flooded with helicopters and low-flying fighter jets. As the two giant CH-53 Super Stallion helicopters maneuvered for a landing location, Scott O'Grady sprinted toward them. Before the second helicopter had time to dispatch its marines, he was on board, and they were off. The actual rescue took less than seven minutes.

Within the hour American F-16 pilot Captain Scott O'Grady was on board the deck of the *USS Kearsarge*, safe and sound.

With not a single man hurt, the TRAP force had pulled off a miracle. I think my sister Stacy put it best in her letter to thank them. The rescue mission, she wrote, was "one moment of perfection in a world of imperfection."

I felt the joy of that miracle as the Super Stallion touched down. Unhooking my lap belt, I stood and moved toward the door. A Marine squeezed the back of my neck with his hand. "Good to have you back," he said, his face shining.

Hopping onto the ship's deck, I broke into a big grin and a brisk trot, with Colonel Berndt's jacket hood flopping behind my head. A bunch of cameras were clicking at me—the first media onslaught—but I didn't stop to pose. I marched straight through a doorway, as directed, and into a crowd of happy, buzzing people. I shook the first hand I could find; it belonged to some Navy lieutenant.

It's hard to describe how I felt—it was as close as I'd ever come to flying without a plane. But even then I was still on guard—still *surviving*—until after I'd been hustled into an elevator with a team of doctors. Only when I reached a ship's hospital bed, to be prepped for a grueling physical, did the last defenses tumble.

*Now* it was over, I thought.

Now I had my life back.[3]

Compared to all of the complex technology around him, his hand-held twenty-eight-ounce walkie-talkie may have seemed too simple, too uncomplicated, too unsophisticated a piece of equipment to call down a powerful armada. His cheap-looking, underpowered survival radio does not appear to be sufficient to effect the rescue of a lost warrior. Compared to high-powered fighter jets, high-tech electronic surveillance aircraft, and multibillions of dollars worth of satellite intelligence, an ordinary communications device may seem too fragile a lifeline—until you remember, the real power is not in the transmitter but in the receiver on the other end.

Prayer: Too simple? Too common? Too uncomplicated?

Too important.

# OUR HOPE
# FOR ETERNITY

# NINE

# The Summit
# of Hope

*And we know*
*that in all things*
*God works for the good*
*of those who love him,*
*who have been called*
*according to his purpose.*
*For those God foreknew*
*he also predestined*
*to be conformed to the likeness of his Son,*
*that he might be the firstborn*
*among many brothers.*
*And those he predestined,*
*he also called;*
*those he called,*
*he also justified;*
*those he justified,*
*he also glorified.*

*Romans 8:28-30*

Just moments before 11:30 A.M. on the afternoon of May 29, 1953, Tenzing Norgay and Edmund Hillary were standing where no other human beings had ever stood. Two-thirds of the way through the earth's atmosphere, at almost six miles above sea level, they stood together at the highest point on earth. At that moment they were literally on top of the world—the summit of the world's tallest mountain, the mountain the Tibetans call Chomolungma. It is the mountain we call Everest.

The expedition led by Sir John Hunt in the spring of 1953 began its formal preparations over nine months earlier. Their meticulous preparation involved eight tons of equipment and supplies, hundreds of sponsors, months of logistical planning, and hundreds of support climbers, porters, and Sherpas. Everest is no place for tourists or sight-seers. Only the fittest and the best prepared can even contemplate placing their feet upon the summit of the highest place on earth.

## THE SUMMIT OF THE SCRIPTURES

In the geography of Scripture, there are many "Everest-like" summits. Among the greatest of these mountains of biblical promise stands the eighth chapter of the book of Romans, with the twenty-eighth verse as its highest peak. The majesty of this verse towers among the mountaintops of the Bible just as Everest towers among the greatest mountains on earth.

However, unlike the daunting challenge facing those who would seek to stand on Everest's summit, no special training is necessary to climb to this summit of biblical promise. It is accessible by anyone who is willing, both novice and expert.

Yet its common access does not mean that what we find here is at all common. Simply because it is easy to reach should not make us underestimate the significance of the view from this pinnacle of passages. This too is no place for tourists or simple sightseers. The challenge of Romans 8:28 is not simply our ascent to it, but our application of it. As with Everest, getting there and living to tell about it are two different tasks.

### The Pinnacle of Hope

Among all of the pinnacle passages of the Bible, why does Romans 8:28 lift us to such a lofty perspective?

The answer is as uncomplicated as it is profound: Hope.

When the faithful employee arbitrarily loses his job and is thrust hopelessly into a marketplace with no work for a man of his age, when the young family next door is brutalized by the sudden tragic death of one of their children, when the respected pastor crashes and burns in a tragic fall from fidelity, when—

—the police officer at the door says, "There's been an accident."

—the doctor says, "It's malignant."

—the lawyer says, "We'll see you in court."

—the teenager says, "If you really loved me, you'd understand."

—the teacher says, "You'll have to do better."

—the person across the desk says, "Maybe next time."

—the woman says, "I can't take it anymore."

—the voice on the phone says, "I'm sorry to tell you this."

—the minister says, "You'd better sit down."

These are the times when we begin to understand the transforming perspective of hope that elevates the promise of Romans 8:28 above the atmosphere of strife in which we live every day.

### The Valley of Reality

Have you been caught up in the swirling chaos of life?

Have you seen the brutality and felt the tragedy?

Are you familiar with the struggle?

Do you know the suffering and the pain?

Have you asked the unanswerable questions?

Then you know what it is that lifts Romans 8:28 above the storms of life.

It is when God seems silent and distant and absent that we best understand what it is about Romans 8:28 that gives us hope. Perhaps this is the climb we must undertake; this is the sacrifice we must make; this is the nature of the struggle to the summit, for without the hardships of life, the vista of Romans 8:28 would lack some of its impact. Just as a climber who has personally experienced the cost of the climb appreciates best the view from the summit, so too the weary believer who has felt the cold sting of the harsh winds of life appreciates the value of this vista of hope.

Romans 8:28 promises all who climb to its summit a perspective that everything we encounter, feel, and experience is working according to God's design. There is a design in this darkness; there is a purpose in this chaos; there is meaning in the catastrophes of life. When there are no answers nor explanations, we can climb to the summit of Romans 8:28 and find hope.

## WHEN QUESTIONS GO UNANSWERED AND GOD SEEMS SILENT, WE HAVE A COMFORTING HOPE

Christie would have been twenty years old today. I am writing this chapter on February 29—leap year day. Even though I never met her, I came to know her very well. Christie was remarkable not only because she was born on a day that is only recognized once every four years, but also because of her love of life and her love for people. Everyone who knew her told of her vivacious spirit and her boundless energy. She was an excellent student, a model daughter, and a helpful companion to her young single mother. By all accounts, she was a delight.

One warm February afternoon in Dallas, Christie asked her mom if she could go across their small apartment complex to play with a friend. With her mother's permission, Christie kissed her good-bye and headed out the door. It was the last time her mother ever saw her precious nine-year-old.

For the next two years, her mother never gave up hope that Christie would be found. She combed police reports and traveled across the country where people claimed to have spotted her daughter. She spent countless hours in support and comfort of others who had lost children. After two years the police contacted Laura with a report of the discovered remains of a child about Christie's age found in a field just miles from her home. Two days later the medical examiner confirmed that it was indeed her missing daughter. The search was over, but the questions remained.

### WHAT DO YOU KNOW?

Romans 8:28 begins with "we know." The word used here is οἶδα (*oida*).[1] Of the words in the New Testament for "to know" or "to gain knowledge," οἶδα (*oida*) implies more than any that this is something we can understand or something we have the innate ability to know.

The word comes from the same root word as εἶδον (*eidon*), which means "to see." In this sense the implication is that we can *see* that all things work together for good. We may not fully comprehend how God works, but according to Romans 8:28, we can *"see"* that He does.

## FLIGHT LESSONS

A number of years ago I visited a large cattle ranch with some family friends. This beautiful ranch sprawls over many acres of the southwestern Nebraska plains. In order to manage so large an operation, my friend's stepfather Cal (who just so happens to be an ex-air force fighter pilot and general airplane guy) kept a couple of airplanes at the nearby airport. When we went to visit, he asked me if I would like to fly around the ranch with him one afternoon. I eagerly agreed. What was in store for anyone gullible enough or perhaps insane enough to go for a "ride" with Cal was unknown to me then.

When we arrived at the small community airport, we went to a hangar where Cal showed me his beautiful twin-engine Beechcraft Baron. He told me that he flew this plane to Lincoln and other places around the state for cattle auctions, family outings, and Nebraska football games. The Baron had twin engines, a beautiful paint scheme, plush comfortable seats, and curtains in the windows. This would not be the plane we were flying today, however.

As we closed the doors of the Baron's hangar, we dragged open the next set of hangar doors. Cal explained, "I don't use the Baron to fly around the ranch. Too expensive. I prefer to use this—the *Citaborea*."[2]

As he told me this, I looked into the hangar at the high-wing, tail-dragging, bright yellow airplane that looked as if it were constructed mostly out of paper products, and I said, "Oh . . . good."

If I had any doubts about the trouble I was in, they were confirmed when we pulled the airplane out of the hangar. It was lighter than some of the lawn mowers I had pushed in my life, and I had never flown in one of those. Without so much as a glance at my expression, Cal opened the airplane's door. (I use that term very loosely—as loosely as the door fit. Actually, it was more like the flap of a tent than anything close to a "door.") Then he motioned for me to crawl in.

"Shouldn't you be checking things around the plane first?" I asked as I folded myself into the seat directly behind the pilot. "Kicking the tires or checking the oil or something?"

"Nope. Just hop in, and let's go." Cal fell into the seat in front of me, shaking the entire structure of the plane as he settled in. And with that he reached over and grabbed the poor excuse for a door, fixed the latch, and started the engine.

"Hey, what's that?" I pointed to the small window of liquid sloshing around just above our heads.

"Oh, that. That's the fuel," Cal said out of the side of his mouth. He revved the engine, and we began to roll away from the hangar. "Looks good, right?" It was obviously a rhetorical question, for he gave no indication that my response, either positive or negative, would have influenced our flight plan in any way.

### Take Off

"You strapped in?" Cal called out as we turned into the wind at the end of the runway. I could barely hear him, as the prop wash was filling the cabin with a tornadolike wind that flowed in freely through our bouncing, fluttering, lame excuse for a "door."

At this point I thought of all those luxurious commercial airline flights and all those dreadful, ridiculous, mandatory safety briefings that the flight crews must always rehearse just before takeoff: The instructions about seat backs and safety belts. Those little orange oxygen masks and the seat cushions that can be used as floatation devices. The graceful way that the flight attendants point out the emergency exits. There were no such briefings on the *Citaborea*. That day's safety briefing consisted of: "Make sure that you're in tight—you'll need to be," which in no way eased my mind.

We began to bounce down the runway with the grace of a drunken middle linebacker running across a room full of mattresses. However, it didn't take long before the tail left the ground, and a second later we were up—straight up.

### The Flying Lawn Mower

Over the next few minutes I was treated to a ride that made all the rides at Disney World seem designed for pregnant heart patients with bad backs. First, we flew just off the ground, following the terrain as if we were mowing it. We then flew at eye level directly toward a herd of cattle drinking at a water tank. If this was how they made hamburger in Nebraska, I would never touch another Big Mac. We flew within inches of the cattle and used the windmill next to the tank as a racing pylon, banking ninety degrees as we turned.

"See the cattle there?" Cal cocked his head slightly as he pointed below.

See the cattle? What a ridiculous question. I was close enough *to touch* the cattle. If they had been dairy cows, I could have milked them. The fact was, I was looking straight down at them through *the side window*. The cattle had obviously seen this before, for even though we were low enough to count the number of flies on their backs, they never even looked up from the water tank.

Following this, Cal put the plane into a gentle climb, and we rose high over the ranch and the surrounding countryside. The view was spectacular, with the horizon blending into the thin blue sky in every direction. The town below grew smaller and smaller as we kept climbing. For a moment I relaxed my grip on the frame rails that surrounded my seat. This, as it turned out, was a mistake.

It is impossible for me to say exactly what happened next. All I know is that suddenly the dirt from the floor was falling into my face. This was followed by a series of views of that small town that alternated with views of the pale blue sky—town, sky, town, sky, town, sky, and so forth. One moment I felt as if a giant hand was pushing me down into my seat, and the next moment that same unseen hand was lifting me up by my ears out of the seat. Up, down, sky, ground, right side up, upside down, spin, turn, up, down, sky, town—it went on, and on, and on.

At no point during our flight did I fully understand what was going on. I only knew a few basic things: First, all indications were that I was still alive with each of my limbs still intact. Second, we were still in the air, and as far as I could tell, we had not yet made any unusual contact with the ground. Third, as of this moment, I had not yet thrown up. None of these facts, however, did I consider to be guaranteed forever.

### Look Ma, No Hands!

As you may have figured out, the seating configuration in the *Citaborea* included only two seats, one directly behind the other. Interestingly enough, you could actually fly the plane from either seat. Located with me in the backseat was a set of controls identical to those in the front seat. There was a control stick in the middle, pedals on the floor, and throttle and flap controls on the side. As we were looping and turning and spinning, I could see the stick stirring and the pedals moving.

Even though I could only see the back of Cal's head, I trusted that he was flying. At least, I hoped he was flying. Had he uttered the word "oops" even once, I'm sure I would have lost all hope, along with my lunch. Even though I could barely tell which way was up, I had to place all of my confidence in the hope that Cal knew. I "understood" that he was in control. I could "see" that he was doing something— what, I wasn't sure, but something was keeping us in the air.

## WORKING FOR THE GOOD

Romans 8:28 tells us that we know God works all things together for good. To know or to see that He is in control does not mean we can explain everything that is happening. It does not mean that all of our questions have answers. It does not mean that our lives are always right side up and all we see is blue sky. It does mean that we can have confidence that God is in control even when we are not sure which way is up.

### In ALL Things?

In our text, verse 28 goes on to say that we can know "in all things" God is at work for the good. The Greek word here for "all" is παντά (*panta*). It means exactly what it says: "in all things." In everything— not just some things, not just in the good things, not just in the easy things, but in each and every thing God is at work. This is not that complicated to understand; all means all. That's all.

What is perhaps the most difficult thing to understand and accept about this verse is the next phrase: All things "work together for good" (in the King James translation). How is this possible? We may believe that God is working in all things. We may even be able to see evidence that supports our belief and hope that God is at work in all things— but for the good? In a world filled with heartache, tragedy, unfairness, and injustice, how can we say that all things are working for the good?

Many well-meaning people in times of tragedy seek explanations by pointing out that good things can come from the events. They strive to make some sense of the senseless and give meaning to the meaningless. They point out how families were reunited in the face of trials. They observe that a community was brought together in the wake of disaster. They comment that they themselves took the time to reevaluate their own lives as a result of tragic events. We are naturally inclined to this perspective.

### A Fair Exchange?

In a town near where I grew up, a high school girl was killed at the intersection right in front of her school by a car making a legal left-hand turn. The driver did not see her as she crossed with the green. As a result of her death, the traffic pattern was changed to prohibit left-hand turns, making the intersection safer for the students who crossed there every day.

I remember reading the paper shortly after the decision to change the intersection had been made. One of the people involved commented how important it was for good to come from this tragedy. Changing the intersection meant other lives would be saved. The young girl's death would not have been for nothing.

This is not what God means by "the good." Do you think that the individual who must live the rest of his life with the knowledge that he killed that girl will find comfort every time he sees that traffic light? Do we believe for a second that anyone who sees this kind of exchange, a life for a light, says, "Oh yes, that was worth it"?

The value of the life of a young girl is not equal to a traffic light. That is not God's way of doing math. No parents on earth would be willing to sacrifice their child for a new safety law or some social compensation. You cannot tell me that even witnessing the execution of a criminal who has taken the life of someone you love is a fair exchange.

Even the most swift and final justice, even the most significant change in our society is never truly equal to the loss.

When Romans 8:28 says that all things are working for the good, it does not force us to settle for our human perspective alone. "The good" God is working through all the events of our lives is a good far beyond a human explanation or rationale. In God's equation of justice, the punishment always fits the crime, and the height of the victory always exceeds the depth of the tragedy.

## THE SYNERGISM OF GOOD

The word used in verse 28 for "works" is the word from which we get our English word *synergism*.[3] The dictionary defines *synergism* as "a united action of different agents or organs, producing a greater effect than the sum of the various individual actions."[4] To see the ultimate effect as greater than the sum of its parts is a remarkable insight into the work of God.

The good that God is working does not deny the injustice or soften the tragedy with secondary meanings. With God, tragedy is still tragedy, pain is still pain, and injustice is still injustice. He is weaving the events of our lives into a tapestry, the beauty of which is greater than any single thread can reveal. The good that results will be greater than the tragedies woven in. This is more than making good come from bad; this is turning tragedy against itself, using injustice with injustice to accomplish true justice. He is working all things together for eternal, uncompromising good.

The ultimate example of this perspective is the death of Christ. His death was history's greatest injustice—the only man who did not have to die for His own sin being unjustly executed. Yet by using this injustice, God accomplished ultimate justice. From the dark threads of tragedy, He wove the fabric of forgiveness. This is God's idea of "good." This is the glory of the tragedy of the cross. Christ's sacrifice was the ultimate synergism.

### The Questions Remain

The search for young Christie ended years ago, but the questions remain. Even as I stood at her memorial service and spoke to those who had gathered, I had more questions than answers. Why did she have to die? What does this mean? Why her? Why in this way? Why can't we have more answers?

The questions remain even ten years later. But these questions will not remain unanswered forever. The one thing I knew to be true then—the answer that was a source of hope in the face of so many unanswered questions—is still true today. I know that God is working all things, even the most tragic things, together for good. Christie Proctor was born twenty years ago today, and even though I never met her, my hope was and is this: One day I will.

## WHEN OUR LIVES SLIP OUT OF CONTROL AND GOD SEEMS DISTANT, WE HAVE A CONFIDENT HOPE

One snowy winter afternoon I was returning home from school with my girlfriend and her roommate in the car with me. Common sense and the warnings of the state police prohibited my girlfriend from driving in the hazardous winter weather conditions. Unfortunately these same warnings did not prohibit me.

As we approached the top of a particularly long and steep ice-covered hill, I knew that the best way to negotiate the descent safely was to shift the car into a lower gear at the top of the hill. With all of the experience and skill of my twenty years, I carefully down-shifted and decelerated, and we began to creep down the hill. About one-quarter of the way down this half-mile incline, I boasted to the girls, "No problem," and turned my eyes from the road to take in their awed admiration and approval.

Suddenly the car began to pirouette like a Bolshoi ballerina. I grabbed the wheel and turned into the skid; I pumped the brakes; I stepped on the accelerator; I turned off the radio; I flashed the lights; I prayed; I did everything I knew to do, and yet the car continued to spin with increasing speed down the hill—toward the river at the bottom.

I noticed a number of cars abandoned on the sides of the road ahead. Apparently these drivers had given up trying to negotiate up the hill. Rather than doing something stupid like trying to drive back down the hill and risk winding up in the river, they had parked their cars and walked to their homes at the top of the hill.

At this point I figured we would definitely eventually come to a stop, either by attaching ourselves to one of the parked cars or in the river. Then the car spun around one last time and slid sideways toward the parked cars on the side of the road. I grabbed the wheel. The girls screamed. I signaled my intentions. I closed my eyes. Suddenly the car, facing up the hill, slammed to a stop.

As I opened my eyes, I saw that we had slid sideways directly in between two of the parked cars, with less than a foot to spare both in front and in back. It would have been virtually impossible to parallel-park a car in that space—on dry pavement. Our knotted skid marks cutting through the snow-covered road testified to the wild route we had taken. And yet there we sat, unhurt, mouths wide open, miraculously stopped, without so much as a scratch.

I took a deep breath, put the car in gear, pulled out of the space, and turned back down the hill as if nothing had happened. The girls instantly protested, "What on earth are you doing?"

I turned toward them with a casual lift of a brow and queried, "What? What's your problem? I meant to do that."

The girl in the front seat married me anyway.

## OUT OF CONTROL

Much if not most of life happens to us. When we try to convince ourselves that bad things always happen to someone else, we deny reality. There are many times when our lives seem to be spinning out of control, and we are helpless to do anything about it.

The problem at the root of this loss of control is that we directly attach our hope to this sense of control. When control seems lost, our hope is also in danger. And *this* is truly dangerous.

Are you one of these people?

When the events of your life spin wildly downhill, do you lose hope?

Is your hope only as strong as your grip over the environment of your life and your ability to explain, control, or understand it all?

## GET A GRIP

Romans 8:28 encourages us to look at life differently. From the summit of hope, looking down on life from our God's vantage point, we are encouraged to have a noncircumstantial hope. Whether we are in control or out of control, we can remain hopeful.

As we have seen, Romans 8:28 provides us with a hope built upon our knowledge that God works all things together for good, His kind of good. However, there is a responsibility with this hope. It is a hope that applies only to "those who love him."

This means it is impossible to have hope in God without love for God. Our hope may not be circumstantial, but it is conditional. We control our hope because we control our love. Our hope can grow strong in spite of our weakening grip over our lives because we choose to love God. In this sense we never lose control, and we need never lose hope. The equation then follows: The weaker our grip over our circumstances, the stronger our grip needs to be on Him. Our responsibility is not to control every minute aspect of our lives; our responsibility is to control our love for Him. This we can and should have a grip on.

### Grabbing the Stick

As I sat in the back of the *Citaborea* watching the horizon (as well as my life) flash in and out of my view, I could have easily grabbed the control stick directly in front of me. It was well within my reach. Because I prefer not to be passive in most situations, especially ones involving life and death, particularly my own life or death, grabbing the stick would have been a natural response. However, this would have been a stupid, even fatal response.

As we tumbled through the sky above rural Nebraska that day, there was only one person in that plane who knew how to fly, and it was not me. I barely knew how to be a decent passenger. For me to grab the stick in front of me and begin wrestling with the one person who knew what he was doing would have been beyond stupid—it would have been foolish, moronic, imbecilic, idiotic, and deadly. If I thought it was bad with Cal at the controls, a few seconds of my own aviation skill would have clarified any questions about who should be flying the plane that day.

### Trust the Pilot

I know you get the point. But I also know that we all to some degree fight for control with the one who knows what He's doing. We struggle with special vigor when we feel that everything is slipping wildly past us, skidding and spinning out of control. We wrestle with worry and doubt and fear and anxiety. We stay awake nights and figure and fiddle. We try to fly the plane, control the skid, to do it ourselves. All the while we have only one real responsibility—trust the Pilot.

When God seems distant, He is not. When our lives slip from our control, they are not out of His control. We can have a confident hope not as a result of our circumstances, but as a result of our confidence in the one we love—the one who loves us.

## WHEN WE FACE AN UNCERTAIN FUTURE AND GOD SEEMS ABSENT, OUR HOPE IS COMPLETE

Mount Everest is not really just one big rock stuck in the middle of the Tibetan Plateau; rather, it is made up of many strata, or layers, of different kinds of rock and sediment, each one stacked on top of the other. While not very scientific, we can therefore think of Mount Everest as a giant layer cake. Think of it not as a big solid rock but as the biggest pile of rocks on earth.

### GEOLOGY THEOLOGY

In the verses after Romans 8:28, the apostle Paul gives us a lesson in Geology Theology. What we see is that if verse 28 is the top of the mountain, then verses 29-30 are the strata that lift it to its spectacular height. Just as the summit of Everest sits as the pinnacle of many strata of rock, so too the promise of Romans 8:28 rests upon a solid foundation of different strata of theological, not geological, rock.

### He Foreknew

The first strata of theological promise that forms the mountain of Romans 8:28-30 is the assurance of God's foreknowledge. Foreknowledge literally means "to know before."[5] In Sanday and Headlam's classic commentary on Romans, this term is defined "to take note of, or to fix regard upon."[6] John MacArthur's excellent commentary on Romans adds this insight: "Foreknew is from *proginosko*, a compound word with meaning beyond that of simply knowing beforehand. In Scripture, 'to know' often carries the idea of special intimacy and is frequently used of a love relationship."[7]

FOREKNOWLEDGE. My wonderful wife, Diane, has been pregnant four times. Each time she was "with child," at the first sign that our unborn child was active, she would have me watch and feel for movement.

"Look there!" she would say as I swung around a moment too late to see anything but her hand marking the location of her abdominal tremor. "Here, now, see?" she would cry with exasperation, as if somehow my not seeing this biological phenomenon would make me doubt that there was actually a baby in there. There were many nights when I was instructed to lie in bed with my hand on her abdomen for extended periods of time, like some kind of digital sonar searching for a miniature Loch Ness monster.

I must confess, however, that I never really shared in her enthusiasm for these intrauterine events. I knew that soon enough I would see and feel plenty of movement when I had to change and care for our young child.

Obviously, it is not quite the same for a man as it is for a pregnant woman. While a husband may have strong feelings about his yet-to-be-born child, these cannot compare to the powerful bonding that takes place between the unborn child and the mother. Almost from the moment of conception, a woman not only knows but loves this one whom she has never met.

FORELOVE. I now know how true this is. We never got to meet our first child, and I have since stood and wept at the gravesides of children whose parents never had the opportunity to greet them either. I know of the "love beforehand" that a parent, especially a mother, feels. I know that there is a bond between a parent and a child yet to be born that is as real and passionate as any parent's.

If this is true of us as frail and corrupt human beings, how much more so is it true of God? All the love that an expectant mother feels as she anticipates a face-to-face encounter with her unborn child is but a faint reflection of what Romans means when it says that God "foreknew" us.

Our heavenly Father had a passion for us even before we were born, even before we were formed. He knew what every pregnant mother knows—not only of our existence but of His love for us. This love is not based on anything we might do or become, any more than a mother's love is based upon what this child may be or become. This love exists before our birth, before any of our actions could earn this love. For God to foreknow us is for God to "forelove" us.

### He Predestined

To say that foreknowledge and predestination are deep subjects may be somewhat appropriate, considering our geological analogy. Questions about these two terms that were probably first asked by the original recipients of the apostle Paul's letter have yet to be fully answered. The discussions and theological fistfights that have ensued over these two words are endless. We want to avoid entering directly into this fray by focusing specifically on the implications of these terms as they support our hope.

When we are uncertain of our future, and when God seems unresponsive to our call, inattentive to our needs, or even absent from our circumstances, the promise of Romans 8:29 gives us great hope. For not only did God "forelove" us, but He also "foreordained" us. That is to say, as a logical result of His love for us, He "pre-decides" or "pre-commits" to us. Just as parents love their unborn child, they also pre-decide, as a result of that love, to raise their child.

A parent's commitment is a commitment to love, nurture, raise, support, train, protect, provide, and essentially sacrifice one's life for the child. This commitment is "pre-decided" at conception, whether the parents are ready or not. It is part of the package of being a parent. From the moment you conceive a child, you are a parent for the rest of your life, or you are never really a parent at all.

Once again, if we know this and are able to fulfill this commitment at our best, how much more is this true of God? He never fails in His commitments. He never abandons those He loves. Those He "pre-loved," He also "pre-committed" to bring to eternity and to maturity. The one is a natural result of the other. If we believe that God "foreloved" us, then we can have confidence that He also "pre-committed" to see us through, even when He seems to be absent or inattentive. Parents everywhere know this is true.

A SAILOR'S STORY. It was a typical day for Jesus and His disciples, if any day in Jesus' public ministry could be called "typical." The disciples had been with Him less than two years, but that short time had been filled with a lifetime of activity. They had heard His radical teaching. They had witnessed astonishing miracles. In their private moments together, they had been privileged to hear Him pray and tell, as no other man could ever tell, of the wonder of God Himself.

After this long day of ministry to the large crowd gathered near the town of Capernaum on the northern shore of the Sea of Galilee, Jesus instructed His disciples to get into the boat and cross to the other side of the lake.[8] It had been an exhausting day, and a pleasant evening cruise across the lake would be restful for both Jesus and His disciples.

Sometime during the voyage that night, Matthew and Mark record that without warning a "furious squall" came up on the lake. It was a storm so violent that the boat began to take on water.[9] As the waves crashed over the sides of the boat and the icy spray pelted the struggling sailors, Jesus slept, undisturbed by the ferocious weather all around Him.[10]

Imagine what it would have been like to be there—to be out in the middle of the open sea in a boat barely large enough to fish from, overcrowded with weary men, with only water as dark as printer's ink visible in every direction.

Then without warning the winds begin to stir from a new direction. The scent of the air changes; the temperature drops; the small sails snap wildly against the mast, and the cold black water slaps in an increasingly violent rhythm against the hull of the boat. Within moments the horizon is splintered with bright jagged bursts of lightning, revealing the outline of the muscular clouds overhead.

Almost instantly the stars disappear, and the sky goes black, except where it is ripped apart by the strobes of lightning. The wind now shrieks chillingly above the slapping sea and crashing storm.

The waves no longer slap the boat; they jar it and abuse it, spewing their soaking spray across the heaving hull and into your eyes and nose. The reverberating thunder, the roaring wind, the sandpaper rain, and the writhing boat overwhelm all of your senses. There is furious black sky above you, bottomless black sea beneath you, and no future ahead of you.

Whipped by the lash of the rain, shivering from the sting of the spray, you are clinging desperately with cold white fingers to the tortured craft as it is catapulted from wave to wave. And then in the midst of this tempest you turn to see Jesus sound asleep in the back of the boat.

Most of us would have little tolerance for such a situation. If we are honest, our sympathy goes immediately to the disciples. Most were professional sailors. They were familiar with the fury of the spring storms on this lake, and yet in this situation even they were frightened for their lives. This was no spring shower; it was a life-threatening, sea-churning squall. In their expert opinion, they were in real danger. It was time for some of that supernatural stuff they had been seeing for the past year and a half. It seemed like a good time for the Lord to wake up and help out. They were drowning here.

I can relate to this. When everything around me is black and stormy, my boat is sinking and the squalls of life are beating the stuffing out of me, I figure it's time for the Lord to wake up. This would be a good time for Him to step in and deal with the situation.

Not only did Jesus appear to be unaware of what was going on, but it also appeared that He was completely unconcerned. As the disciples woke Him, Mark records that they accused Him of unconcern: "Teacher, don't you care if we drown?"[11]

HIS PRE-COMMITMENT. Jesus' response is the same in all three gospel accounts. He rebuked the storm, which calmed the sea, and He rebuked the disciples, which confuses us.

Was it such a bad thing for the disciples to be afraid?

Were they wrong to ask the Lord, whom they had seen do other miraculous things, to intervene in their situation?

Were they that far off base when they decided to express their concern, their fear, and their doubt?

Was He simply rebuking the disciples for accusing Him of a lack of concern?

I must admit, I probably would have fared no better.

With the benefit of hindsight, we can learn the lesson without the lashing from the storm or from the Lord. It is the same lesson about the character of God and the quality of His commitments that is taught in Romans 8:29.

When the Lord "pre-commits" to something, He never, ever fails to follow through, no matter how tough the storm may seem. Jesus never said they should get into the boat *and drown* halfway across the lake. He never gave any indication that He would not go with them *all the way* to the other side. Drowning in the middle, storm or no storm, was not in His plan. All things would work out for the good because He had pre-committed to go to the other side. He had given them His word.

### He Called

Family relationships in our day are increasingly complex. Up until the very end of the twentieth century, the child/parent relationship was simple and obvious. Conception led to pregnancy. Pregnancy led to childbirth. Childbirth led to parenting. And it was the parenting that led to the complexities.

For centuries theologians have referred to the five verbs in Romans 8:29-30 as "The Golden Chain." Each idea in these verses is linked directly to and logically follows the others. Just as a geologist can understand why one strata follows the next, so too a believer can understand why each concept in these verses follows another. According to these two verses, it is logical that those whom He loved beforehand, those whom he committed to beforehand, should also be the ones He calls His own.

A ROSE BY ANY OTHER NAME. My oldest daughter's name is Cayah. This is not a family name nor a name that my wife and I deliberated over for months. It is a recovery room name—she should be happy her name is not Demerol or Tylenol.

You see, as we anticipated her birth, we were certain that Cayah was Joshua. We had not even considered girls' names until the doctor informed us that Joshua would be a little awkward for our new daughter. Cayah is a name that I had heard in my Hebrew studies in seminary, and it comes from the Hebrew word *hyh* (*h'y'h*), which means "life." This is also the root from which God's name Yahweh ("I Am") comes. In Israel the name is often transliterated as "Chaya."

While it was not true of us, I know of a number of couples who have been very scientific and thoughtful when naming their children. Those parents considered biblical names, family names, and names that had special significance to them. However, one part of a child's name is rarely open for debate. We certainly had no discussion concerning Cayah's surname—her family name.

There was a time not so long ago that, once children were conceived, they were "called." They had two parents, and their last name would naturally become the child's last name. There was no legal or custodial debate over whose name they would bear, for from the time of their conception, they were identified with their parents. They were members of that family.

The "invitation" of parents to their unborn child to become a member of their family logically follows conception. While this may be complicated in our culture, this is not complicated spiritually. God is not a surrogate birth-parent. Those He has pre-loved, He has pre-committed to, and by this love and commitment He has invited them to become His children—de facto.

Those He loves and commits to, He calls His own. Conception implies invitation. Whether or not this is currently in vogue domestically or scientifically, it remains theologically correct.

### He Justified

Theologically speaking, justification is God's accounting system. We are all born in debt. Our accounts, which we inherit from our ancestors beginning with Adam, have been accumulating a negative balance throughout the history of mankind.

Anyone who understands the compounding of interest will tell you that even a small amount left untouched over thousands of years will add up quite nicely. This debt is passed on from generation to generation, and no one is exempt from this ancestral obligation. In fact, the debt is so large that all of the efforts of all of humanity are unable to erase it. It is a debt of eternal proportions. Essentially, all men are born hopelessly bankrupt according to the ledger of God. No one's actions, no matter how noble, no matter how pure, no matter how virtuous, are able to erase the negative balance of even one individual.

One day an Individual who possessed unlimited wealth entered the marketplace of humanity. He was eternally rich in virtue, purity, and holiness—the currency of heaven. He came and walked among us, making His wealth available to any of the human debtors who would apply for His aid. His generosity knew no bounds. His resources knew no limits, for He possessed an account accrued not merely with the interest of human history, but with the compound interest of all eternity. According to God's accounting, this one, His one and only Son, had the capacity to pay the debt that we, as human sons and daughters of debtors, could never pay. This is the story of our salvation—our debt wiped clean by the gift of Jesus Christ.

This, however, is not the full story of justification. For not only was The One Who Came willing to reduce our obligation to God to zero, but He was also willing to assign to us the fullness of His wealth. He eradicated the totality of our debt, and He then took our name and placed it over all of *His* accounts. The balance of accounts written in God's account book, also known as "The Book of Life," has our names written down as holders of the account of "the righteousness which is in Jesus Christ." The account book of God not only shows the absence of debt in our accounts, but it also shows the presence of an unlimited wealth of righteousness under our name. When the ATM of heaven spits out your account balance, there will be no limit on the "amount available" line. This is justification.

Justification is a done deal. Completed. Finished. The check has cleared. The full transaction has been accomplished. As members of God's family, His children have a guarantee of this exchange of wealth. But if you remember your account history, it took three days for the check written on the cross to clear.

### He Glorified

In the original language, all five of the strata that make up the structure of these verses are in the Aorist tense. In koine Greek, the Aorist tense indicates a completed past action, often with effects stretching into the present. We can easily understand that the previous four theological actions (foreknowledge, predestination, calling, and justification) were certainly accomplished in the past. But according to Romans 8:30, glorification has already been accomplished as well. We may have difficulty understanding how this can be true.

## TWO-DIMENSIONAL LIVING

When the apostle uses the Aorist tense, he is expressing his confidence in something yet future by describing it as if it were already completed. He is so certain of the completion of these actions that he can speak of them as if they have already been accomplished. But what does all this mean to us right now?

That we are already glorified does *not* mean that Christians glow in the dark or that we have more "glory" in life than anyone else. That we are already glorified does not allow anyone to claim superiority in holiness.

What it *does* mean is that God has already glorified us in this life by saving us. Just as the other five strata primarily reflect God's character, so too we see great glory in our redemption. The fact that He made the sacrifice to have a relationship with us brings Him great glory. His sacrifice on our behalf has already brought Him great glory.

As we struggle with the uncertain future, when God seems distant and unreachable and heaven is silent to our questions, our hope is built upon not just what He is doing in our lives, but on what He has already done. We need not rest upon our limited understanding of what God is doing right now; our hope stands firm upon the rock strata of all that God has already completed.

## CLIMBING TO THE SUMMIT OF HOPE

I had been cutting steps continuously for two hours, and Tenzing, too, was moving very slowly. As I chipped steps around still another corner, I wondered rather dully just how long we could keep it up. Our original zest had now quite gone and it was turning into a giant struggle. I then realized that the ridge ahead, instead of still monotonously rising, now dropped sharply away, and far below I could see the North Col and the Rongbuk glacier. I looked upwards to see a narrow snow ridge running up to a snowy summit. A few more whacks of the ice-axe in the firm snow and we stood on top.

My initial feelings were of relief—relief that there were no more steps to cut—no more ridges to traverse and no more humps to tantalize us with hopes of success. I looked at Tenzing and in spite of the balaclava, goggles and oxygen mask all encrusted with long icicles that concealed his face, there was no disguising his infectious grin of pure delight as he looked all around him. We shook hands and then Tenzing threw his arm around my shoulders and we thumped each other on the back until we were almost breathless. It was 11:30 A.M.[12]

In the years since Hillary and Norgay stood on top of Mount Everest, fewer than 600 people have made the summit, and more than 140 have died trying. Every year between forty and fifty expeditions attempt the climb. On one day in 1993, forty people made the summit. On the weekend in May of 1995 when eight people lost their lives on the mountain, there were a total of eleven expeditions within 2,900 feet of the top.

Yet of those who make it, no one lingers there. At any extreme altitude above 18,000 feet, human life is in a losing battle against the elements. Hillary and Norgay stayed on the summit a total of fifteen minutes before they had to begin their descent. Still, those fifteen minutes changed their lives forever. Some forty years later, Hillary remembers their impact:

When I look back on it all there is no doubt that reaching the summit of Everest on 29th May 1953 was a major turning point in my life. . . .

As we trekked from the mountain back to Kathmandu my innocence was quickly dispelled. Every day mail runners were meeting us with masses of telegrams and newspaper cuttings indicating the immense impact the climb had universally made. When I was finally handed a letter from John Hunt addressed to "Sir Edmund Hillary" I was horrified but reluc-

tantly forced to realize that my life, and indeed the lives of all
the expedition members, had irrevocably changed.[13]

## TRANSFORMED BY HOPE

Those of us who know Jesus Christ know how our lives can be changed
by one event, even one moment. So too as we stand on top of the
promises of Scripture, our perspective of life—even life itself—can be
transformed forever. This is how the view from Romans 8:28-30 ought
to affect us. We may linger there long and often, but as we return to
travel through the valleys of life, we ought never to forget the panorama
of God's provision we have seen from this spectacular summit.

# TEN

# The Roller Coaster of Hope

*What, then, shall we say in response to this?*
*If God is for us,*
*who can be against us?*
*He who did not spare his own Son,*
*but gave him up for us all—*
*how will he not also,*
*along with him,*
*graciously give us all things?*
*Who will bring any charge*
*against those whom God has chosen?*
*It is God who justifies.*
*Who is he that condemns?*
*Christ Jesus,*
*who died—*
*more than that,*
*who was raised to life—*
*is at the right hand of God*
*and is also interceding for us.*

*Romans 8:31-34*

It is called the Dragon Kahn. Designed in the 1990s by the firm Bollinger and Mabillard of Mothey, Switzerland, it was built at the Port Aventura amusement park in Salou, Spain. If you are willing to risk your life on it, you will travel over three-quarters of a mile—4,166 feet, to be exact—on a two-inch steel track that will send you upside down almost as much as right side up. The Dragon Kahn will toss you around, throw you up and down, and invert you eight times—more times than any other roller coaster in the world. It is at this time considered to be one of the world's most challenging complete-circuit, multi-element steel roller coasters.

Roller coasters are cool. Whether we are talking about the Steel Phantom at Kennywood Park in West Mifflin, Pennsylvania, which drops 225 feet into a ravine at over eighty miles per hour, or the longest roller coaster in America, The Beast, at Paramount Kings Island in Cincinnati, Ohio, with its 1.4 miles of track, 800 feet of tunnels, and its stomach-turning 540-degree-banked helix. You may not think riding one of these contraptions is a lot of "fun," but I do. I am one of those the-lights-are-on-but-no-is-home, not-quite-right-in-the-head kind of persons who thinks being scared out of your mind on a roller coaster is a great diversion and something worth paying money to do.

### THE ROLLER COASTER OF LIFE

While I think roller-coaster riding is cool and fun as a diversion, it is not how I want to live. The neck-pounding you take on the large wooden Texas Giant at Six Flags Over Texas in Arlington, Texas, makes it a nice place to visit, but only a total melon-head would want to live on it. The rush of dramatic drops and turns is fun for a while, but it would get rather tedious, not to mention punishing, if you had to make your home on a roller coaster.

Since living a roller-coaster life is no fun, why is it that we often live our lives on what seem like emotional, relational, and spiritual roller coasters?

Why do we constantly rise to a picturesque summit only to descend with reckless speed into an emotional hairpin turn?

Why are we so often up one day and down the next?

It cannot be because we like it. It cannot be because we want it. It cannot be because we think this is how God designed our lives to be lived . . . is it?

### The Summit Plummet

Many a believer has experienced a Romans 8:28-like summit, only to free-fall into a valley of discouragement not long after. It seems that too many times our mountaintop experiences are followed by crashing and crushing tumbles into defeat. It gets so that our once-hopeful outlook is tainted with the expectation of a following decline. Then, as a sort of self-fulfilling prophecy, we experience an emotional bungee-jump, making our experiences feel far more like painful trials than joyful triumphs.

### Stranded on the Dragon Kahn

It seems to be an unending cycle, an endless Dragon Kahn. Following the fall, the dutiful Christian eventually climbs back to the mountaintop, returning to the summit of hope and promise, once again experiencing the optimistic perspective from another spot of high ground. A weekend retreat, an encouraging meeting, or an uplifting time of personal study can return the believer to the rare air of peace. Yet for most of us, it does not seem to take long before the rope breaks, the pinnacle of peace gives way, and the avalanche of reality forces the Christian mountaineer back down into the valley once again.

This mountaintop/valley cycle, or as I like to say, the summit-plummet syndrome, is the roller-coaster ride of life. We all know about it. We all have lived it. Unfortunately most of us consider this bungee-cord lifestyle to be normal, unavoidable, and a typical part of the fabric of life. We assume that the topography of the Christian life is filled with unavoidable peaks and valleys, and, for the most part, we believe that we are destined to live in this relentless pattern. Apparently not only does pride come before a fall, but so do weekend retreats, spiritual successes, and times of joy, peace, and hope.

### THE BELAY OF HOPE

As we have seen, Romans 8:28-30 is a summit of hope. It is a passage of unsurpassed encouragement. But because we go there does not mean that we must now descend into hopelessness. Paul certainly does not. Almost as if to prevent our imminent fall from hope, in the very next verse he tightens the line to secure us with one astonishing insight: *"If God is for us, who can be against us?"*

To use mountain-climbing vernacular, this could be called a *belay*. When a climber fastens his rope to a rock or to a climbing device such as a piton or a carabiner to keep himself from falling, he is using a technique called *belaying*. When another person secures a rope for a climber and holds it if he falls, he is said to be *belaying* the climber. Romans 8:31 is our *belay*. Paul sets our rope almost as if he anticipates that following the truth of Romans 8:28-30, we would be expecting to fall. Why should this be?

## THE POWER OF HOPE

Genuine hope by its very nature is stable. It is reliable, dependable, and unchanging. Genuine hope gives us confidence when nothing else in life can. Genuine hope is built upon a foundation of truth and of certain expectation. Genuine hope is solid and secure. Genuine hope must therefore have as its source unchanging, eternal truth.

False hope, on the other hand, is temporary, transient, imaginary, and unreliable. This kind of hope is often manufactured by humans and founded on circumstances. The vapor of hope can infiltrate a life through the smallest of opportunities and the slightest of dreams. Imaginary hopes and false hopes often appear to be as powerful as genuine hope itself. This elixir of half-hope can be traded by any motivational snake-oil salesman or religious vagabond, and people will buy it, for in a land of hopelessness even a false hope seems better than no hope at all.

## THE SYMPTOMS OF FALSE HOPE

Even a half-hope can empower and transform a hopeless life. Yet this very power indicates the danger of hope. The power of hope can be easily misrepresented or misused. Hope can be falsified and counterfeited with ease. To some, Saddam Hussein is a source of hope. To others, Charles Manson is a messenger of hope. It is the power of hope that explains the influence of a man like Adolf Hitler.

The roller-coaster lifestyle is symptomatic of a life built on false hope. The acquisition of a half-hope and the depression that follows its failure produces the emotional, relational, and spiritual roller-coaster ride. False hope never lasts. It causes the torturous twists and turns of life that toss your perspective back and forth like a rag doll on the Texas Giant.

When the addicted gambler places his last dollar on the table, he has a hope.

When the devout mystic chants over the body of a loved one, he has a hope.

When the desperate teenager risks self-destruction for the sake of acceptance and popularity, she has a hope.

When the lonely single mother agrees to marry a man she hardly knows, she has a hope.

When the terminally ill patient agrees to a desperate and unproven course of treatment, he has a hope.

When the frightened toddler clings to her favorite blanket as the timpani of thunder shakes her windows, she has a hope.

Romans 8:31 catches us before we fall. Before the pattern of repeated summit-plummet takes hold, the apostle secures the rope and stops the ride: *"What, then, shall we say in response to this? If God is for us, who can be against us?"*

## THE NEED TO NEED

He came into my office yesterday brokenhearted. I had never seen him so depressed. In spite of his excellent education, good looks, and wonderful personality, he felt like a complete failure. It's strange how "love" can do that to someone. Relationships like this are often a ticket for an extended ride on the Dragon Kahn.

"I just have no confidence," he repeated like a mantra as he stared hypnotically at my carpet. "I don't know what to do. My career is going nowhere. I feel terrible, and I don't know how to make it all stop. What should I do?"

To listen to him, you would think he was a lonely kid whose dog had just died or that he was some sort of penniless vagrant, a tourist lost in a foreign land, a homeless refugee with no food and no friends, a bum who had just spent his last dollar on some cheap wine and would spend the night sleeping in the gutter. But in reality he was a healthy, intelligent, well-dressed, well-paid professional—with a broken heart. He was falling fast into the black hole of hopelessness because the one thing he believed he needed to survive, he could not have.

"I need her. I need to know what to do," he said over and over as he apologized for sounding so stupid, being close to tears.

## OUR HOPE HELD HOSTAGE

The summit-plummet often takes hold when we feel as if our needs are unmet. When our desires remain unsatisfied and our expectations are unfulfilled, it is easy to lose hope. The descent can be rapid and deep when we are overwhelmed with the feeling that we can never fulfill our needs and attain our dreams.

Many of us as modern men and women tie our hopes to our dreams of success and accomplishment. We even use the terms *hopes* and *dreams* as synonyms for success, and by so doing, make our hope but a vapor, completely vulnerable to our circumstances, as insecure as a blind date. We must be careful that our hope is not held hostage by our dreams.

It is common for us to attempt to belay this fall from hope with optimism, creative thinking, or even denial. This is why credit cards were invented, so that our needs, desires, and expectations could be met *right now*. The fall into hopelessness is belayed by an instant fulfilling of our unmet desires. We just charge it. Yet when the bills pile up, we find that this rope is far from secure. All of this is simply a half-hope, a hope "placebo."

With a change in perspective and transformed priorities, we can begin to put the brakes on the roller coaster of life. It is a question of knowing the difference between what we really *want* and what we really *need*.

## THE NEED WE NEED

According to Romans 8:32, God will meet the needs of every believer: *"He who did not spare his own Son, but gave him up for us all—how will he not also, along with him, graciously give us all things?"* This is the confident expectation of a genuine hope.

But how does this work?

I am a believer, and I still have unmet needs. My young professional friend is a believer, and his unmet need is crushing him in an emotional vise. I can tell you with some confidence as I encounter the wreckage from the struggles of godly men and women that there are a lot of unmet needs out there.

But are these our real needs?

Read Paul's rhetorical question again. His question reveals the nature of our genuine need. Not only do we realize God's willingness to meet our needs sacrificially, but most importantly, we see that *in His Son* He has already and will always meet our needs. That is to say, "in Christ" God will meet all of our needs.

I do not want to sound like an exegetical Houdini who explains away what seems to be a straightforward scriptural promise, but this verse *does not mean* that all of our fantasies, dreams, and desires will be fulfilled by God. This verse promises us that *in Christ* we have all we need, for *in Christ* God has met our greatest need. The problem is not that we have unmet *needs* but that we have unfulfilled *dreams*, and we cannot tell the difference between the two.

### Our Greatest Need

This is the responsibility of a loving parent. Loving parents seek to know the difference between their child's perceived needs and the child's real needs. My children "need" candy, or so they tell me every time we are in the supermarket. My children "need" to rent a movie, watch cable TV, buy new shoes, have a new stereo, and they each tell me that they "need" to be an only child. If they had all these things, so they say, their needs would be met.

What do my children or any children really need? First, they need loving parents. Without loving parents, they could have all of the candy, toys, movies, and things a child dreams of, and yet their greatest need would be unmet. In essence, this is all they really need; everything else is just what they want. Our heavenly Father has demonstrated His love for us in an unparalleled fashion. In Christ we have the secure affirmation of our Father's love, and *this* is our greatest need. Everything else is simply what we want.

In spite of our theological and spiritual posings, this truth is not easy for us to accept. This simply doesn't seem to be enough. It is difficult for the woman whose husband has just told her that he no longer loves her, and he's moving out to accept the idea that all she really needs is to know that God loves her.

It is difficult for the family whose father is dying of cancer to accept the idea that all they really need is to realize that they are loved by God. It is difficult for any of us whose lives are being blown apart to really be satisfied with the simple confidence of God's sacrificial love for us. However, it is also not easy for my daughters to accept that their most important need is simply for my love. The difficulty does not make it wrong. We need to ask ourselves one question: Are we really willing to say that Christ is *not enough* and that we need more?

### Everything but Hope

Pretend for a moment that you had every desire you could imagine: Aladdin's three-wish lamp. The winning lottery ticket. Unlimited wealth, power, beauty, health, influence, and popularity. Every dream, every fantasy—but no love. No promise of eternal life. No confidence in forgiveness, justice, or heaven. Would you have genuine hope?

This is the essence of the truth we have seen in Romans 8:24: *"But hope that is seen is no hope at all. Who hopes for what he already has?"*

So why then do we attach our hope to things?

Why do we tie our hope to people, positions, and power?

These things, even in infinite amounts at their most consistent and in the best of circumstances, cannot meet our greatest need. Our greatest need is not financial. It is not physical, emotional, relational, psychological, or political. Our greatest need is spiritual, and Romans 8:32 promises us that this need, our greatest need, has already been met.

Many years ago my family received a Christmas card with words something like these written on its cover:

*If our greatest need were financial,*
  *God would have sent us an economist.*
*If our greatest need were for conquest,*
  *God would have sent us a general.*
*If our greatest need were for information,*
  *God would have sent us an educator.*
*If our greatest need were political,*
  *God would have sent us a politician.*
*If our greatest need were technological,*
  *God would have sent us an inventor.*
*If our greatest need were physical,*
  *God would have sent us a doctor.*
*If our greatest need were for pleasure,*
  *God would have sent us an entertainer.*
*But our greatest need is spiritual,*
  *So God sent us a Savior.*

My friend is coming to terms with his unmet needs. He is following in the footsteps of the rest of us who are learning that our hope is secured not in our circumstances but in the promise of God's sacrificial love. He is learning that this is his greatest need and that this need has been fully met.

This doesn't mean that he feels nothing for his lost relationship. This does not mean that his desire has diminished. It simply means that he has not lost touch with the source of genuine hope.

When we find ourselves trapped on the roller coaster of life, Romans 8:32 reminds us that the feelings of disappointment and discouragement dragging us down may be due to confusion about the one thing we really need. It is easy to understand the reason for this confusion. We live in a world that does not appreciate God's provision and has no confidence in His promise to meet our most important need. We may live in a roller-coaster world, but we do not have to live like it.

## THE NEED TO PLEASE

He was labeled a heretic and an enemy of the church. He spent the last four years of his life in academic and theological exile. His friends and followers were driven from their teaching positions, ministry appointments, and some even from their homeland. He was condemned by the religious leaders of his day and criticized by official church councils and tribunals. He was stripped of his professorial and pastoral tenure, and his writings were declared to be heretical. Even after all this, the church felt that they had not sufficiently punished him. Forty-four years after his death, they exhumed his body, burned his corpse, and threw the ashes into the Swift River.

## WYCLIFFE: THE REBEL OF RIGHTEOUSNESS

What had John Wycliffe done that made the established church so angry as to dig up his dead body and burn it? Had this Oxford professor of theology led an immoral lifestyle? No, the religious leaders of his day were actually quite accepting of this kind of moral weakness within their ranks.

Had he sought to embezzle funds from the church in the name of salvation? No, this indiscretion was also widely accepted by Wycliffe's peers. So what had John Wycliffe done to infuriate the religious establishment of his day?

He taught people the Bible.

Wycliffe began to expose hypocrisy among his peers and to speak out against some of their unbiblical practices. He had the audacity to suggest that the Bible, not the church, was the final authority in the life of the believer. He began to write extensively about his radical theological ideas and against church practices that he believed to be unscriptural. In the years before his death, he translated the Latin Vulgate version of the Bible into English, making the Bible available to people outside of the priesthood. It was for such offenses as these that Wycliffe was condemned as a heretic.

John Wycliffe was undoubtedly familiar with Romans 8:33: "*Who will bring any charge against those whom God has chosen? It is God who justifies.*" We do not know, however, if he scratched his head when he read it. We do not know if this verse was going through his mind as he was forced to sit silently through a series of manufactured accusations at a tribunal called by William Courtenay, the bishop of London, at St. Paul's Church in 1377.

We can only imagine that he wondered how this verse applied to his life as he was marked a heretic by the pope himself and the archbishop of England in 1378. Wycliffe certainly translated the verse into English, but we do not know exactly how he translated it to his own life.

### Ambushed by Antagonism

There is perhaps no more difficult situation in life than to be falsely accused. At some time in our lives, most of us have shared an experience of being charged with some action, attitude, or motive against which it is impossible or pointless to defend ourselves. (If you never have experienced this, you obviously have never had teenage children.) These are certainly some of the hardest times in life.

According to the promise of Romans 8:33, our appeal is to God and not to men. When Paul asks the rhetorical question, *"Who will bring any charge against those whom God has chosen?"* we want to answer, "Anyone and everyone." But before we can respond, he answers his own question: "It is God who justifies." In this he is reminding us that our guilt or innocence is only secondarily a matter of man's opinion; it is primarily a matter of God's opinion.

What others think or believe about us ought only concern us after we first consider what God thinks. False accusations, lies, and rumors may abound around us, but they carry no real weight before the throne of God. We may be accused and attacked in the judgment of others, but the only verdict that really matters is handed down in the courtroom of heaven by the one and only Almighty Judge.

He knows our hearts. He knows our motives. He knows our secrets, and nothing is hidden from Him. When the false accusations and lies are cutting us to shreds, we stand or fall in the court of the only one who really matters, and He is the one who justifies.

### IN THE HANDS OF HOPE

The roller-coaster ride of life can dive and turn violently as others' opinions rise and fall about us. When we are surrounded by applauding admirers, when their hot air of adoration fills our lungs and their praises lift us into the stratosphere, we can reach a lofty mountaintop of self-esteem. But as soon as the praises fade and the criticisms mount, the descent begins.

### Blue Monday

However, the wounds from false accusations are not just inflicted by the words and attitudes of others; they can also be self-inflicted. Our own guilt, our own self-pity, and our own tendency to compare ourselves with others can wind up shooting us in the foot. We do not need an angry boss, a jealous coworker, or a stubborn church board to inflict false accusations on us; we can often do it just as well without their help.

Most pastors resign on Mondays. The high that comes from a powerful Sunday sermon, the adoration of a loyal congregation, or the attention and affection of an exhilarating hour of worship are most always followed by the deafening silence of a Monday morning reflection. I know. I've been there.

A pastor's blue Monday is not due to beginning a new work week but to realizing the futility and frailty of his efforts the day before. "Who was missing this week? Why do I bother? No lives are really ever changed. The offering was inadequate; the board is still angry and belligerent, and all but three people fell asleep." The applause is never enough. The praises never last, and there is a fear that even the most flattering of compliments are laced with insincerity. These wounds are self-inflicted.

### Healing Self-Inflicted Wounds

This is how our hope is lost. We become too concerned with the opinions of men, even when those opinions are our own. We too desperately want to please people. Their perspectives and their praises, or the lack of them, shape the hills and valleys of our confidence, and our hope is tied to these attitudes. We are held hostage by the fickle whims of public opinion when our primary concern ought to be the opinion of God.

There is only one Critic whose review of our life matters. There is only one Judge whose ruling will determine the destiny and value of our lives. There is only one whom we must satisfy—and He is the one who justifies.

Perhaps you are stuck on the Dragon Kahn of hope because you are focusing your life and your confidence on the opinions of others. You are lashed to the applause and praise of people. You are held hostage by your own need to be accepted and approved by others. You are certainly not alone. Pleasing people has value—the admiration of others is undoubtedly satisfying. But we ultimately stand or fall before only God. We must seek to bring praise and satisfaction to just one. Getting off the roller-coaster ride requires living with just one audience to please, and He knows the truth, no matter what anyone else might say.

## AS DEAD AS WYCLIFFE

It seems somewhat humorous to picture the religious zealots of Wycliffe's day digging up his long-dead body. To imagine their anger as they tore into the dirt that had covered his grave for almost half a century gives us a vivid image of the irrational nature of most false accusations. We can imagine that they cursed at his corpse and rebuked the rotting shell that once was John Wycliffe. The picture is both absurd and analogous to those who falsely accuse or criticize the innocent.

It is appropriate for us to consider ourselves as dead as Wycliffe when his adversaries stood piously beside the fire that consumed his skeleton. Was Wycliffe himself in pain that day? Did he feel the wrath of his enemies or the heat of their anger? Did he suffer for one second as they set a torch to his decaying clothes and to his decomposed body? Of course not. He knew none of it. For even as his enemies shouted out their accusations, he was seated in heaven with the one who knew the truth. He was already in the courtroom of eternity with the one who justifies. Even as his body went up in flames, he was as secure as any believer in the arms of his Savior and Judge, untouched and unscarred by the heat of their anger.

## THE NEED TO SEE

Between 1905 and 1932 a number of world-renowned physicists such as Albert Einstein, J. J. Thomson, Ernest Rutherford, and James

Chadwick constructed theories that described the nature of the atom. Even though they could not "see" an atom, the mathematical evidence provided by these and countless other physicists has caused the world to believe in the existence of atoms. While they could not *see* an atom, they were confident that these invisible atoms were the building blocks of the universe.

## SEEING IS BELIEVING

We live in a world where seeing is believing. Missouri's state motto could be our credo: "Show Me." We watch instant replays of sports action over and over in slow motion from a variety of angles, and even then we do not always accept the official verdict. We expect incontrovertible empirical evidence to be presented before we will believe.

### More Than Meets the Eye

But this is intellectual hypocrisy. We know that things happen in the universe that we cannot yet explain, and we also know that things happen that we cannot yet see. Every reasonable man of science must admit that in the decades to come, the ever-increasing knowledge of our universe will make what we know today seem positively infantile.

Even the atheistic scientist must believe in some things that he cannot prove and agree to the existence of things he cannot see. Quarks, neutrinos, dark matter, photons, and even protons and electrons existed before anyone had proof of their existence. To oversimplify the case, if we are honest, we must admit there is more to this universe than meets the eye.

This is the essence of hope—there is more to life than meets the eye. A genuine hope "sees" more than we can see with our eyes or prove with our instruments of science. If the mass spectrometer, the particle accelerator, the electron microscope, and the Hubble space telescope are some of the tools that we use to see the unseen in our universe, then the Bible is also a tool we can use to see the unseen.

### Life Through the Lens of Hope

Romans 8:34 may sound like some hollow theological rambling until we consider it as a spiritual electron microscope showing us what we cannot see with our own vision. When we read Romans 8:34, we are looking through a lens into a spiritual dimension invisible to the naked eye.

This verse asks another rhetorical question: *"Who is he that condemns?"* Paul answers, *"Christ Jesus, who died,"* and then he provides us with a significant look through the magnification of a scriptural lens: *"More than that, who was raised to life—is at the right hand of God and is also interceding for us."* With this insight, the lens of Romans 8:34 reveals something important about our universe—something that goes on beyond our vision, outside of our view.

With the same judicial tone as in verse 33, Paul poses a question of legal sovereignty and authority: "Who's in charge here? Who has the final say?"

The answer is the same person as in verse 33: Jesus Christ—not the one who justifies, but the one who condemns. In these two statements, Paul affirms that forgiveness and judgment come from the same person. This is our hope. There are no committee decisions about our eternal destiny. No cantankerous despots can cast us into condemnation. No thumbs-up or thumbs-down seals our fate according to the whim of the crowd. The one who died for us is the one who has the authority to convict us, and if He died for us, how could He sentence us to pay what He has already paid? With this verse we see that the entire chapter of hope has now come full circle: *"Therefore, there is now no condemnation for those who are in Christ Jesus."*

### The Magic Bullet

It seems almost as an afterthought in the last half of verse 34 that we are exposed to an ongoing unseen truth: *"More than that, who was raised to life—is at the right hand of God and is also interceding for us."* This inspired insight affirms that our hope has not only been secured in the future, but even right now, our hope is being secured in ways that we cannot see. Jesus Christ not only died for us, but He also lives for us.

Not only is there more going on than we can see, but it is happening on our behalf. What else in life is like this? Without our effort, energy, involvement, time, or money, someone is looking out for us. It is a grand conspiracy of eternal dimensions.

## A *Conspiracy of Hope*

Conspiracy theorists abound in our day. If there is one grand conspiracy of which we can be certain, it is that there is a conspiracy of conspiracies. There are people who believe in government conspiracies, international banking conspiracies, and intergalactic alien conspiracies. You can find sensible men and women who believe that everything from cable television to unleaded gasoline are the products of smoke-filled room conspiracies.

Many people are convinced that every area of life is infected by covert groups of evil individuals whose sole mission in life is to destroy everything and rule the world. The United Nations, the Trilateral Commission, the FDA, FBI, CIA, DEA, EPA, NEA, ATF, IRS, and any other government organization identified by three letters (under the umbrella of the acronym conspiracy theory) are all considered by some people to be the "real" powers pulling the strings of this world.

Whether or not these theories hold water or simply cause us to sweat unnecessarily is a matter of endless debate. Some theories are certainly more valid than others. But common to virtually all of these conspiracy theories is the belief that someone or something is behind the scenes, pulling the strings and working to make our lives miserable.

### BELIEVING IS SEEING

Romans 8:34 lets us in on an unseen conspiracy. Without our knowledge, permission, or control, there *is* Someone pulling strings and making things happen. Behind the closed doors of heaven where microscopes and mathematics cannot look, there is a heavenly conspiracy. In the incense-filled corridors of the throne room of God, Jesus Christ is at work. He is at the right hand of the Creator of the universe, using His position and power to whisper into the ear of God Almighty. He is constantly, clandestinely weaving a conspiratorial web that we cannot see or even at times detect.

When we begin to slide into discouragement because everything seems to be falling apart, when we find ourselves tumbling into anxiety and despair because all of the evidence indicates that our lives are hopeless, when all of our instruments of science, physics, and medicine show that our condition is critical and deteriorating, we have an unshakable hope.

## Ride Over

Cedar Point Amusement Park is located on the banks of Lake Erie in Sandusky, Ohio. It opened for business in 1870 and began operating its first roller-coaster ride, the Switchback Railway, in 1892. Since then Cedar Point has become the roller-coaster capital of America. At this time the park contains eight different roller coasters, representing what coaster aficionados hail as the most comprehensive lineup in the world.

Cedar Point has roller coasters that run right side up and then turn you upside down. They have rides that hang upside down and then turn you right side up even though you are hanging upside down. They have roller-coaster rides that run on wood, steel, and wood-and-steel combinations.

The Magnum XL-200 is an "out-and-back" steel roller coaster that is anything but traditional. Designed by Arrow Dynamics and built in 1989 for eight million dollars, it was listed in the 1990 *Guinness Book of World Records* as the world's fastest roller coaster with the world's longest drop. The first hill of the Magnum XL-200 climbs 205 feet above the ground and then plunges 194 feet at a sixty-degree angle, making it the steepest roller coaster in the world and allowing the train to reach a speed of seventy-two miles per hour, making it one of the fastest roller coasters in the world. Then there is a *second* hill that drops riders from 157 feet and curves just in time to avoid Lake Erie. Along the way are three tunnels with special sound and lighting effects. The track is just short of a mile long (5,106 feet), and the ride time is two and a half minutes.[1] What a ride!

I have never been to Cedar Point Amusement Park, although my daughters and I would love to go there someday. I have never ridden on the Magnum XL-200. I have never been to Port Aventura in Salou, Spain, to ride the Dragon Kahn or to Paramount Kings Island to ride The Beast, the longest roller coaster in America. Nor have I been to Kennywood Park in Pennsylvania to ride the Steel Phantom. Maybe someday.

But I have ridden the roller coaster of life. I have sat in hospital waiting rooms to hear news of tragedy. I have been in the boss's office to hear the news of termination. I have ridden the ups and downs of marriage and parenthood. I have been tossed around, turned upside down, and hung out to dry. I have been at the summit, and I have been in the valley. I know what it is like to be up one minute and down the next. I know the queasiness in the pit of my stomach and the ache in my heart. I have been on that ride.

Have you been to the valley of despair where everything seems hopeless?

Have you been upside down, inside out, and tossed around?

Do you know this ride?

Is this your life?

Life will always have its ups and downs. Part of the adventure of life includes these peaks and valleys. There will always be days of joy and days of sorrow, times of praise and times of pain, moments of triumph followed by moments of tragedy. Life is not a flat, straight, well-paved interstate on which we travel to heaven with the cruise control on. Life is bumpy and twisty and neck-straining.

But our hope is not. We do not need to be tossed and turned mercilessly even when life throws its worst at us. Our hope secures us. When our emotions would run away with us and our hearts would cast us down, we have a hope that is tied to solid rock.

Ask yourself one last pair of questions:

If God is NOT for us, who is?

And if God is for us—who can possibly succeed against us?

Ride over.

# ELEVEN

# The Standing Ovation of Hope

*Who shall separate us from the love of Christ?*
  *Shall trouble*
  *or hardship*
  *or persecution*
  *or famine*
  *or nakedness*
  *or danger*
  *or sword?*
  *As it is written:*
  *"For your sake we face death all day long;*
  *we are considered as sheep to be slaughtered."*
*No, in all these things*
  *we are more than conquerors*
  *through him who loved us.*
*For I am convinced that*
  *neither death nor life,*
  *neither angels nor demons,*
  *neither the present nor the future,*
  *nor any powers,*
  *neither height nor depth,*
  *nor anything else in all creation,*
  *will be able to separate us*
      *from the love of God*
      *that is in Christ Jesus our Lord.*
                              *Romans 8:35-39*

My wife, Diane, and I bought our first home after ten years of marriage. Thanks to the generosity of many friends, we finally found ourselves in a wonderful house, one far nicer than we could ever have imagined. We were overjoyed with the prospect of putting down roots in our own place. It is part of the American dream, and we were excited to see it come true for us.

I am not sure that I am excited anymore. Being a homeowner is a pain. The foreboding clouds of taxes, insurance, and mortgage payments constantly hang over our heads, and there is always something that needs fixing, painting, cleaning, or replacing.

Sinks clog up, water heaters leak, air conditioners break, paint peels, carpets rip, lights burn out, and the grass (read: *weeds*) just won't stop growing. Our fantasy family castle has become an unstoppable monster, a black hole of projects, a money pit with an ever-multiplying punch list of unfinished tasks. It is impossible to own a home and not have something on the to-do list. If it's not broken, it's breaking; if it's not breaking, it needs cleaning; if it's not dirty, breaking, or broken, it's new. Give it time.

My view of all of these domestic maintenance problems and the relentless battle of upkeep on everything from automobiles to toasters is perhaps an exaggeration; however, the reality it reflects is easily explained. There is a natural, physical, scientific law that explains these problems—we all learned it in high school physics class. It is called the Second Law of Thermodynamics.

### Running Down and Falling Apart

The Second Law of Thermodynamics is one of the fundamental laws governing the scientific understanding of our physical universe. Very simply, this law states that within a closed system that is in an ordered (low entropy) state, conditions will tend to move spontaneously toward a state of maximum disorder (high entropy). This is illustrated by the fact that clocks run down—they do not wind themselves. Likewise, a warm drink in a cold room cools off, and a cold drink in a warm room warms up.

The Second Law of Thermodynamics also explains why that wonderful new house you just bought starts to fall apart the day after you move in. When you build a building, it starts to decay as soon as you are finished. It does not continue to build itself. Scientifically, this is called the tendency to achieve equilibrium, but we informally call it running down and falling apart, and everybody's doing it.

## The Reign of Chaos

In some sense, almost everything in the universe is subject to the Second Law of Thermodynamics, from intergalactic star systems to water heaters. Just about everything goes from organized to chaotic if left to itself. This may even explain why our children do not pick up their toys. Without some sort of outside intervention, everything in life decays, rusts, rots, falls apart, dries up, piles up, runs out of gas, or dies. If you doubt this, try not washing your hair or changing your baby's diaper for a month and see if there are not significant signs of entropy.

This principle is particularly true when we think in spiritual terms. If left unmaintained and undeveloped, an attribute such as hope will eventually decay into hopelessness. An individual who does not receive regular reasons to hope will eventually lose all hope. A family or a society given no reason to hope will wind up without it. Without regular encouragement, without a consistent and reliable reason to have hope, an individual, a family, or a society loses its energy and begins to break down.

### THE GIFT OF HOPE

It is also the principle of the Second Law of Thermodynamics that the state of entropy within a closed system can only be changed by influences from *outside* of that system. This is true of hope as well. Just as a baseball cannot find within itself the energy to throw itself, and a falling-down home does not have the energy to fix itself, so too a hopeless person cannot find genuine hope within himself. Optimism, fantasy, and dreams can come from within us, but genuine hope does not come from within us. Genuine hope must have an external source. Genuine hope is given, not generated. Genuine hope is no more found within an individual or a family or a society than the energy to get to the green is found within a golf ball. Unfortunately, the last place we look is often the best place to find hope.

## THE LOVE OF HOPE AND THE HOPE OF LOVE

In these final verses of Romans 8, this message of hope is carved in the solid-stone character of Jesus' most inspirational attribute—His love. This is not a sentimental examination of a romantic attraction. These verses are not simply an emotional imaginary portrait of a fictitious sovereign. Set before us in these words is a vivid panorama of the greatest love mankind has ever known. And it is within this vista of our Savior's love that the finale of our hope is best viewed.

What is it that makes the love of Jesus so powerful, so solid, and so inspiring?

How can this love be so strong as to overpower the laws of nature and not only maintain our hope but energize and revitalize it?

What are the characteristics of a love that never runs down, runs out, or runs dry?

Romans 8:35-39 closes our study of hope like a standing ovation. The applause of all of mankind echoes between the lines of these verses. On the day when every knee will bow and every tongue will confess,[1] these words will find their symphonic realization on the lips of those He loved. It is here that we find three characteristics of the unparalleled, unsurpassed love of Jesus, the spectacular finale of our hope.

### A LOVE MORE CERTAIN
### THAN ANY ADVERSITY

It is often said that there are only two things certain in life: death and taxes. However, it seems to me that there is one more certainty in life: trouble.

Romans 8:35-36 depicts this life of trouble in high-contrast black-and-white images: *"Who shall separate us from the love of Christ? Shall trouble or hardship or persecution or famine or nakedness or danger or sword? As it is written: 'For your sake we face death all day long; we are considered as sheep to be slaughtered.'"* In this portrait of His love there are no shades of gray, no ambiguity or doubt—only dark trouble set in stark contrast to one bright hope.

## THE RULE OF LIGHT

The brilliant promise of the Savior's unfailing love is set like a diamond against this velvet backdrop of trouble. This eternal promise shines like a precious and flawless gem as it is laid against the bitter guarantee of "trouble or hardship or persecution or famine or nakedness or danger or sword." It is here that the rule of light applies to our lives and our hope: "The blacker the darkness, the brighter the light."

This darkness is not simply a possibility; it is a certainty. There are no "ifs" included in this stormy landscape of life. Struggles are a part of this world, a part of life. Count on it. Trouble is here to stay, because we live in a dark and dangerous world.

## THE GREATER THE STRUGGLE, THE GREATER THE STRENGTH

The sevenfold catalog of trouble in Romans 8:35 reflects not only the apostle Paul's personal experience but also the common experience of all men. The first three terms, "trouble," "hardship," and "persecution," reflect situations that confront every human, not just a first-century apostle. They refer to the dark days of anxiety and grief, discouragement and defeat, suffering and injustice. To be stressed out, pressed down, pushed around, and beat up is not simply an ancient struggle; it is a timeless battle. These three terms offer a snapshot of life in the nineties—A.D. 90 or A.D. 2090.

The next two terms, "famine" and "nakedness," reflect intense physical need. While many of us may never experience genuine famine or total financial destitution, we are familiar with the difficulties of life that place us in physical need. The sour taste of suffering lasts long after our needs are met, and it is a bitterness best not soon forgotten.

### Trouble with a Capital T

The final two terms in this grocery list of difficulties are even more strikingly prophetic regarding the apostle himself than the previous troubles. With an inspired autobiographical foresight, our personal guide through the land of hope predicts that we will never know separation from the love of our Savior even when we experience danger and the sword. In a little over ten years from the time he wrote it, this would become a brutal reality in his own life.

The book of Acts records Paul's Roman imprisonment; however, the record ends before he is released. Church tradition tells us that after two years under house arrest in Rome, Paul was finally released around A.D. 62. If the word *danger* describes anything, it describes Paul's perpetual status as a fugitive and later his status as a visiting convict in Rome.

Even more poignantly, church tradition tells us that following his release, Paul continued to travel throughout the Roman Empire for another five undocumented years, until some time around A.D. 67. At that time the Roman Emperor Nero had the apostle arrested again and returned to Rome, where he was charged with treason. Then some time between A.D. 67 and 68, he was put to death—decapitated by sword.

Not coincidentally, the final word in Paul's catalog of life's catastrophes is the autobiographically prophetic term μάκαιρα (*makaira*), the word sometimes used for an assassin's or executioner's sword.

### The Prophecy of Pain

We do not know if the apostle realized the prophetic nature of his words. It is not hard to imagine that as the soldiers pushed his matted hair aside to expose his prison-stained neck, his words, the words of Romans 8, were directed to them. As the executioner fixed his eyes on the block and, with one violent sweep of the μάκαιρα (*makaira*), ended the apostle's life, I like to believe that these very words were on Paul's lips: "*Neither danger nor* μάκαιρα (*makaira*), *shall separate me from the—*"

At that instant, before his final breath had even escaped his lungs, in the flash of an eye, his hope was turned to reality, and his faith was turned to sight. With the word *love* still on his lips and the flowing robes of righteousness instantaneously gleaming over his shoulders, he was embraced by the one who had never, and would never, let him go.

### The Forecast Calls for Pain

In those times when life puts the "squeeze" on us, we are tempted to imagine that we are in greater danger than we actually are, to the point of ruin. I prefer to imagine that the squeeze does not come from my circumstances but from Jesus' grip. It is when I am most pressed that He holds me tightest. When the stress and the pressure are greatest, so is the reminder of His love. We could say it this way: The tighter the squeeze, the stronger His grip.

Scholars may debate the exegetical nature of this love, whether the love we shall never be separated from is our love for Christ or His love for us. To some degree the argument is moot; if we are never separated from it, then the responsibility for it is not in question. If a child runs to her father in the midst of a raging storm, who is holding the other tighter? Whose love is the first? Whose love matters more?

Yet in this symphony of hope, in this crescendo of commitment, it is His love that is certain, certainly not our love for Him. His love for us is guaranteed. Our love for Him comes because, first and always, He has loved us. We hold on tight because He holds us tight.

## THE GREATER THE ADVERSITY,
## THE GREATER THE ASSURANCE

I have often had conversations with people who question the existence of God with the argument, "If there is a loving God, then why is this world so rotten?" They often ask with sincere skepticism, "How can a powerful God allow so much evil in the world? How can your God let innocent babies die? Why does your God allow evil people to prosper and innocent people to suffer? Why doesn't God, if He exists, put a stop to all this bad stuff? If God is love, then why is there so much pain in my life and in this world?"

You would hardly think that an answer to these inquiries is found in the almost depressing words of Romans 8:36: *"For your sake we face death all day long; we are considered as sheep to be slaughtered."* But it is.

Romans 8:36 is about the transforming power of the hope of heaven. It is a vivid reminder that we are not to fall in love with this life, for *"we face death all day long; we are considered as sheep to be slaughtered.*" Since we are sheep headed for slaughter, this world holds for us no real promise, no real satisfaction, and no real hope. Every day only brings us closer to the day of our destiny, the day of our execution.

One of the reasons God does not prohibit evil in this world is so that we might not grow too attached to this place. This world is not our home; it is neither our destiny nor our final destination.

### Imagine This

In 1971 one of the most influential songwriters of the day, John Lennon, wrote a moving peace anthem titled "Imagine." It remains one of his most popular and elegant pieces of music. According to Lennon's worldview, expressed repeatedly in "Imagine's" lyrics, the world would be a better place—if there were no heaven.

If there were no heaven, so he believed, then people would have to make this world heaven. In John Lennon's theology, without heaven we would stop wasting our lives and start making the world a better place. If we just understood that this is all there is, we would no longer be confused or in conflict. We could make this world heavenly. This was his hope.

Apart from the sociological and historical evidence that indicates a society with no final accountability will increasingly demonstrate a lack of responsibility, John Lennon's hope for heaven on earth does not take into account one great problem: adversity.

### Imagine That

*Imagine all the people living life in peace* . . . when suddenly a tornado swoops down on unsuspecting families, depriving innocent children of a chance at life and devastating a family's lifetime of labor. *Imagine* everyone standing on a hilltop holding hands and singing (as they were in an old Coke commercial) . . . while in another part of the world an earthquake ravages a community and caves in homes as people lie sleeping in their beds.

*Even if* every individual on earth were somehow motivated to consider every other individual as more important than himself for no other reason than that he ought to, planes would still crash, buildings would still burn, babies would still die, and diseases would still strike.

Even in a perfect world, this is not a perfect world. Tragedy can reach out from the unknown and strike down the innocent without a human being lifting a finger in anger, and in the end everyone still dies anyway. Imagine that.

## A LOVE MORE SATISFYING THAN ANY VICTORY

Romans 8:37 is one of the most triumphant verses in the entire Bible: *"No, in all these things we are more than conquerors through him who loved us."* The concept of being *"more than conquerors"* is as hope-filled a concept as the Scriptures have to offer us. But what exactly does it mean?

The term ὑπερνικάω (*upernikao*) literally means to "over- conquer." It means more than simply to triumph in battle or conquer in a contest. The combination of the prefix ὑπέρ (*uper*) and the word νικάω (*nikao*) results in a form of hyperbole or splendid exaggeration, so it can be understood to mean "to hyperconquer." This compound word implies that through the love of Christ we gain more than a military or athletic victory. It literally means what it says; we do more than simply conquer. Being a "hyperconqueror" is to gain a victory far more spectacular, more sensational, more stupendous than any human could achieve. It is a supernatural victory.

### THE THRILL OF VICTORY

One of the greatest moments I have ever witnessed in sports history took place on the evening of October 18, 1977. It was the seventh game of the World Series. The New York Yankees and the Los Angeles Dodgers were locked in a three-game-apiece tie. The winner of this one game on that cool October night in New York would be the World Champion; the other team would be—just the other team.

Among all the great players who entered that contest, one stood above the rest. His name was Reggie Jackson. It was that night in New York that sealed his place in the fall classic legend, for in this game

Reggie hit three consecutive home runs, almost single-handedly winning the World Series.

I remember watching the game as if it were yesterday. Each time the pin-striped number 44 walked to the plate, there was an expectation that he would send the ball out of the stadium. On his final turn at bat, he hit the game-winning home run, a laser shot to dead centerfield. Reggie seemed to simply will the ball out of the park. He made it look that easy. I collapsed in awe.

As I watched him stride around the bases amid the crowd's pandemonium, I felt that to be Reggie Jackson at that moment would be the greatest thing on earth. To be the dominant player on the winning team was as good as life could get. Everywhere he went, he was the hero. Life could not possibly get any better.

Do you remember that moment? I am sure a few of you do, but probably most of you don't. After over twenty years the glory of that moment has faded. The memory has been eclipsed by other great athletic victories. The problem with human victory is that it fades over time. The faded memory of victory is often all that remains long after the contest ends. This, however, is not what Romans 8:37 means.

In this verse, we are promised a supernatural victory. It is the everlasting, unending, undefeated love of Christ that makes us "hypervictorious." We are more than conquerors, for we have a victory greater than the greatest human victory. In His love we have a victory far superior to anything else we will experience, a victory that will never tarnish, spoil, or fade. The thrill of any human victory eventually wears thin; there are always other heroes, other battles, and even losses. No one stays on top forever, and there is nothing that can never be outdone, except for one thing—the love of Christ.

His love is greater than any victory because it never ends. The results of the triumph of His love will never fade or wear thin. The praise of those who know His love will never be silenced, and those who are victorious in Him will never be defeated. This is what it means to be a hyperconqueror: To know His love is more lasting and more satisfying than even the greatest human victory.

## WINNING IS EVERYTHING

The famous Green Bay Packers coach Vince Lombardi is reported to have made famous the saying, "Winning isn't everything; it's the only thing." This is no more true of anything than it is of death.

How do we win in dying? There is only one way to win in dying—by being in Christ. When Romans 8:37 promises us that in Christ we are hyperconquerors, we have the promise of more than victory over adversity or tragedy. We have the promise of leaving life undefeated. To be a hyperconqueror is to conquer death itself. In this, our hope is secure because of a love more satisfying than any victory. When death loses, everyone in Christ wins. In Him we are hyperconquerors because His victory was the world's greatest selfless victory.

## A LOVE MORE POWERFUL
## THAN ANY ADVERSARY

At the dedication of the Cathedral of the Redeemer in the Kremlin in Moscow in 1882, Piotr Ilyich Tchaikovsky publicly performed for the first time his composition *The Year 1812*. The composition and its famous overture were written to commemorate the Russian defeat of Napoleon and his retreat from Moscow in 1812 seventy years earlier.

One of things that makes this piece of music so memorable is that Tchaikovsky incorporated a military band and cannon fire into the finale of his overture. In the original score, along with the parts for the strings, horns, wind instruments, and percussion, there is a part for *field artillery*.

The apostle Paul was also a master composer, and the finale of his symphony of hope is accentuated by his verbal cannon fire. Verses 38 and 39 are the final measures of his composition, ending his masterpiece of hope with poetry and power. Like the blasts from Tchaikovsky's cannons, the apostle lights up the sky with staccato promises building to an emphatic climax. It is perhaps the greatest crescendo in all of Scripture. To use the vernacular, he "blows us away."

> *For I am convinced that neither death nor life—BOOM—*
> *neither angels nor demons—BOOM—*
> *neither the present nor the future—BOOM—*
> *nor any powers—BOOM—*
> *neither height—BOOM—*
> *nor depth—BOOM—*
> *nor anything else in all creation—BOOM—BOOM—*
> *will be able to separate us—BOOM—BOOM—*
> *from the love of God—BOOM—BOOM—BOOM—*
> *that is in Christ Jesus—BOOM—*
> *our Lord—BOOM—BOOM—BOOM—BOOM—KA-BOOM!*

## THE ADVERSARIES OF HOPE

As the smoke clears, we can see the enemies of our hope lined up against us, standing silhouetted, backlit by the love of Christ. In poetic array, ten adversaries stand between us and genuine hope.

### Dead or Alive

In the fall and winter of A.D. 48, Paul was on his first missionary journey. He and Barnabas were having a successful ministry in the Asian cities of Lystra, Iconium, and Derbe. Their ministry in Lystra was so successful that the people there thought these men were the Greek gods Zeus and Hermes. The crowd began to call them gods and wanted to offer sacrifices to them. This was not that peculiar, considering that a man who had never walked a step in his life was jumping all over the city of Lystra after Paul had simply told him to do so.[2]

Paul and Barnabas possibly had found an elevated place where they could speak to the people who began to gather in response to the miraculous healing of the lame man. The missionaries stood at the center of the crowd in the middle of the busy plaza, trying to convince the curious mob of their simple humanity and of Christ's deity. Yet with every word the two men spoke, the scene grew more confusing and frustrating.

The crowd soon began to fragment into informal discussion groups of individuals who were reacting to these two strangers. The people listened to Paul and Barnabas speak in Greek, but they were soon whispering to one another in their own Lycaonian dialect.

Fathers spoke to their children and pointed toward Paul and Barnabas. Husbands leaned over to cup their hands over the ears of their wives and tell them what was going on. Neighbors and friends shared their opinions with one another. What had begun as a swarm of whispers was becoming a stampede of conversation. The garbled noise of the crowd grew overpowering, and soon Paul and Barnabas could barely be heard above the verbal melee.

"We've had to deal with these two before. For the sake of our families, we had to drive them out of our cities, Antioch and Iconium." One voice had caught the attention of the people.

Just then another spoke out: "They were dividing our families, turning neighbors and friends against each other. They were not concerned with the good of the community. They are nothing but traitors and troublemakers."

Another righteous-sounding voice shouted through cupped hands, "They are heretics and liars! Demon worshipers! Evil men! Deceivers! They tell lies and harm our children." With the infection of anger spreading through the crowd, it was not long before the people grew fevered.

By now there were dozens of voices. The once-whispering, fragmented crowd now ebbed and flowed with one violent voice. Then finally a stone flew. Then another and another. The first ones found their mark. Soon stones and rocks were bouncing off of Paul's forearms and glancing off the side of his head, thumping like drumbeats on his exposed chest and back.

As Paul and Barnabas jumped down from their podium, the crowd parted before them like the Red Sea. Women grabbed their children, and men ran from the incoming or deflected stones. The crowd drew back quickly as a shower of stones rained on the two men. Soon the escaping crowd had formed a dusty ring around the two defenseless missionaries.

Paul and Barnabas were now cowering together in the middle of the open gash in the crowd. Each man was futilely defending himself from an ever-increasing hailstorm of rocks. The most hostile of the men and women pressed their way to the inside edge of the crowd, where from a few feet away they unleashed their assaults. Their curses and missiles could hardly miss their target.

Barnabas was soon lost in the moving sea of assailants. The wrath of the crowd became myopically focused on Paul, the lone staggering apostle. His final steps were punctuated with a barrage of stones. As he fell onto the pavement, the angriest of them stood over his fallen body, casting down their stones again and again as Paul lay defenseless on the pavement. His body convulsed at the impact of each rock.

"There! He's dead," someone, gasping in anger, cried out as he delivered the final blow. With that, the crowd lifted his lifeless body from the street and dragged him from the city. They left him lying by the side of the road and filtered back into the city.

Perhaps some of the young men boasted as they rehearsed their cowardly heroism. Others may have shook their heads as they considered the brutality of what they had just seen. Mothers may have attempted to explain to their impressionable children why things like this had to be done to men like that. But most of them probably returned to their activities, their thoughts drifting somewhere between enthusiasm and shame.

LEFT FOR DEAD. Some of the frightened disciples in the crowd had found Barnabas. Following in the wake of the violent mob, they had made their way with him out of the city to the roadside where the apostle's body was lying. They had been unable to intervene, helpless to stop such an incensed melee. They had been forced to stand by and witness Paul's execution. Now, as they gathered around the bruised, motionless body, there was only confused silence and sorrow.

A number of theologians believe that the apostle Paul actually died that day in Lystra. The crowd thought he was dead because possibly he was. The reason these scholars believe Paul died is due to something he mentions in his second letter to the church in Corinth:

> I know a man in Christ who fourteen years ago was caught up to the third heaven. Whether it was in the body or out of the body I do not know—God knows. And I know that this man—whether in the body or apart from the body I do not know, but God knows—was caught up to paradise. He heard inexpressible things, things that man is not permitted to tell.[3]

Apart from some chronological difficulties with the probable date of the second Corinthian letter and the date of the events at Lystra, this makes for an interesting possibility. Still, even if the apostle did not actually die at the hands of the mob in Lystra, we can affirm that he had a really bad day. If he did not actually die and experience a vision of heaven, he probably wished he had.

Whether Paul personally experienced what he records in 2 Corinthians, we cannot say for certain. But we do know from the book of Acts that he came closer than most of us ever have. So when he writes in Romans 8 of his learned confidence that nothing in life or death can separate us from the love of Christ, we can say with certainty that the man knows what he's talking about.

THE LIFE-AND-DEATH STRUGGLE. Can life attempt to separate us from our hope? It certainly can. The events of life do not need to be as brutal as the events in Lystra to be just as hurtful.

Do you know the pain of life?

Have you been beaten down, dragged around, and left for dead?

Do you know how harsh the "mob" can be?

We don't have to feel the physical sting of stones to know what pain is. We can know the hurt that comes when those around us turn on us to hurl their insults. Life can and does sometimes hurt—a lot.

Can death try to separate us from our hope?

We may absolutely feel that death robs us of our hope. As we stand at the graveside of someone we are certain we cannot live without, or as we mourn for someone whose loss is unjust, tragic, or untimely, we may strongly feel that death can separate us from our hope.

But Paul knows better, and so can we. If nothing in life can separate us from our hope, then neither can anything in death. In the totality of our condition, whether alive or dead, full of life or feeling like death, there is not one thing—absolutely nothing in this world or after it—that can separate us from the love of Jesus Christ our Lord. No matter the condition, no matter the situation, no matter the circumstances, we can have hope. Dead or alive. Take it from someone who knows: His love is greater than any adversary—even the adversary of death.

BOOM.

## Principalities and Powers

The second pair of our adversaries are neither impersonal nor circumstantial; they are personal and real—with personality and identity. They not only stand against us, but they are aggressively determined to destroy us.

HELL'S ANGELS. There are angelic powers that seek to separate us from the love of Christ. It is highly unlikely that these would be the "good guys." They are fallen angels, the demonic armies, the agents of Satan.

We make a grave error in our thinking if we believe that demonic forces are imaginary, mythical, or benign. They are powerful and real, and they have but one mission—to separate us from the love of Christ. They may be self-deceived, but they are not confused. They hate God and the people of God. They do not sit passively and watch God's people coast into heaven. They have only one agenda, which is to destroy our hope—yours and mine. They have no other goals to confuse their priorities.

Satan is the greatest author of deception in all of creation. He is so complete in his deceptive ability that he has even deceived himself. He and his legions of messengers believe that God will ultimately change His mind about their judgment and that He will do so because of you and me. Satan believes that if enough people are condemned to eternal punishment, the mercy and grace of God will ultimately overpower the justice and holiness of God. If the corridors of heaven are empty and the gates of hell are overflowing, then the love of God must cancel out the holiness of God, and God will have to recant on His judgment, thus allowing Satan to assume the throne of God.

In this hypothetical scenario, we are the bargaining chips, and our faith and hope are Satan's worst nightmare. With one agenda in mind, the legions of Satan's army will do anything to keep us from the love of Christ. They will do anything to destroy our hope. There is no plan B. You and I are their primary, secondary, and only targets.

Have you ever wondered why it is so difficult to live by faith?

Have you ever considered how much easier it is to fill your mind with doubt and despair than with confidence and hope?

This is no accident.

A supernatural conspiracy orchestrates the mind-set of a society against God. The current of culture does not flow toward God; it rushes in the opposite direction. Twenty-four hours a day, seven days a week, 365¼ days per year, Satan hates you. He takes no days off, and he commissions his messengers to destroy every shred of validity in your life of faith.

But can these "angels" separate us from the love of Christ?

Can these agents of deception overpower the love of God?

Are the powers of darkness able to put out the light of hope that anyone can find in Christ?

Not according to Romans 8. The most desperate, deceived, and determined supernatural angelic force cannot take us from His hand.

THE ARCH DELUXE. The second of our powerful pair of adversaries are the ἀρχή (*archāi*), which is often translated "rulers." In most cases this term is used by Paul to describe evil authorities and rulers, most of whom are supernatural. But it can also be used to describe earthly rulers and human authorities. If the first of the two terms, "angels," refers to the spiritual authorities that hinder our hope, then it seems appropriate that this second term may be the natural authorities who would stand against us.

Is it possible that those with human authority hinder our hope?

Can political leaders do so?

Can those in positions of power in business do so?

Can people who have influence in our educational system block us?

Could religious leaders who fail to live worthy of their calling hinder our hope?

Do leaders in the media, the arts, or entertainment promote negative influences on our faith and our hope?

Wake up and smell the coffee. At times it seems as if their agenda is as clear as that of demons.

Even in the face of this much antagonism, we need not withdraw in fear. These angels and rulers, the highest powers in heaven or on earth, cannot and will not ever be able to separate us from the love of Christ.

BOOM.

### Back to the Future

A woman sat in my office the other day and said, "If I just knew how all this is going to turn out, I could get through it." She was facing uncertainty in her marriage, which made her relationally, financially, and emotionally insecure. She expressed what many of us feel when we do not know what lies ahead. Our confidence hits the skids. Our hope has limits. We feel we can hang on—as long as it is not for too long. If we could see light at the end of the tunnel, we think we could hang on a little longer.

Patience and persistence are the allies of hope. When we become impatient and inconsistent, we open the back door for the adversaries of our hope—the things of the present and the things of the future. It is easy for us to imagine how these adversaries can separate us from our hope.

Have you ever been in a difficult or stressful situation that you thought would never end?

Have you ever had to wait far longer than you ever imagined for resolution, provision, healing, security, or comfort?

Do you know what it is like to feel so distant from God that He seems absent from your life?

Have you faced obstacles so overwhelming that their sheer enormity overpowered any hope you had of getting through?

Have you ever found yourself in a hole so deep that you could not see the top, and you were ready to give up all hope of ever climbing out?

Do you know about these financial holes, medical holes, relational holes, and spiritual holes?

Then you know of the adversaries of time and space. We all know them and are familiar with their power to erode our hope. Too familiar.

In the Christian life there are no spiritual crystal balls or biblical fortunetellers. We are not given the inside information on the twists and turns of our daily lives. We do not know when the good times will come or how long the hard times will last. There are no verses in the Bible that tell us what day or month we will find a new job or when or if our broken marriage will be restored or at what hour our prodigal child will come home.

Things present and things to come have the power to stand against our hope. There are days and circumstances that can cause even the most faithful and determined believers to search for the light at the end of the tunnel, only to find themselves staring into the headlight of an oncoming train.

There are times when the struggles and the trials seem to pile on top of us, one after another, tragedy upon tragedy, heartache upon heartache. It seems just when we are the weakest and the most vulnerable that we often bear the heaviest load. There are also those times when the answers come too slowly, when the gates of heaven seem closed, and the voice of God seems silent.

All of these struggles are real. All of these trials are painful. Every day of unanswered prayer is a day too long. Every hour with a broken heart is sixty minutes more than we can bear. But can these things separate us from our hope? Can the loss in any single battle change the outcome of the war? Not when we know who wins. We know what happens in the last chapter; we know who wins the war. And we know the one who knows. We "know not what the future holds," but we "know who holds the future," and He holds our hands.

BOOM.

## The Prize

The word *dynamite* comes from the Greek root word δύναμις (*dunamis*), which literally means "power." The image of a dynamite explosion vividly illustrates the original Greek word for the last enemy of our hope listed in Romans 8:38. Without making too much of this analogy, we are reminded that no power, whether natural or supernatural, whether explosive or corruptive, whether chemical or spiritual, can separate us from the love of Christ.

We could think of our hope as a sort of heavenly Nobel prize. Those who receive it as a reward have held on to their faith in spite of the "explosions" in the fields of physics, chemistry, medicine, literature, economics, and peace. It was written in the will of the Savior that those whose hope conferred the greatest benefit on mankind will be awarded this prize.

## It's in the Stars

The final pair of adversaries standing against our hope (forming the bottom part of the power lunch) are the words *height*—ὑφωμα (*hypsoma*) and *depth*—βάθος (bathos). These words were sometimes used in secular Greek as astronomical and astrological terms, referring to the location of stars on the horizon. The Greeks believed that the positions of the stars affected a person's future. It is the same thing some confused people in our day believe; they call it a horoscope.

A refugee from the 1960s might say these have "good vibes, good karma" or "bad vibes, bad karma, man." This verse implies that all the nonsense of horoscopes, biorhythms, palm readings, and other astrological mumbo jumbo has no capacity to separate us from our genuine hope in the love of Jesus, no matter what is predicted for us. We have hope regardless of how our "stars" are aligned.

A more straightforward way to understand the words *height* and *depth* is in terms of distance, both literal and figurative. If the first pair of terms in our power lunch sandwich represents the adversary of time, then these terms can represent the adversary of space.

In an almost literal sense, this means that there is no location on the earth or in the universe where we are apart from God, separated from Christ's love or without hope. There is really no such thing as a godforsaken place. There is no physical place where we might find ourselves too distant, too high, or too low for His love to reach us.

The author of Psalm 139 understood this truth.

> *Where can I go from your Spirit?*
> *Where can I flee from your presence?*
> *If I go up to the heavens, you are there;*
> *   if I make my bed in the depths, you are there.*
> *If I rise on the wings of the dawn,*
> *   if I settle on the far side of the sea,*
> *even there your hand will guide me,*
> *   your right hand will hold me fast.*

Psalm 139 also provides us with an application only implicit in Romans 8:39: Christ's omnipresent love means that there is no place in heaven or on earth, not even within our hearts, that precludes His presence. His love brings us hope that not only comforts us but also compels us to purity. He knows the heights and depths of our character. He is with us in the most profound and the most debased of our thoughts. It is a testimony of His forgiveness and a motivation for our holiness. In this our hope and our holiness are related.

> *O LORD, you have searched me*
>   *and you know me.*
> *You know when I sit and when I rise;*
>   *you perceive my thoughts from afar.*
> *You discern my going out and my lying down;*
>   *you are familiar with all my ways.*
> *Before a word is on my tongue*
>   *you know it completely, O LORD. . . .*
> *Search me, O God, and know my heart;*
>   *test me and know my anxious thoughts.*
> *See if there is any offensive way in me,*
>   *and lead me in the way everlasting.*

While we know we are never beyond the reach of God's love geographically and theologically, at times in our lives we may feel this is not true emotionally or spiritually. Both the heights and the depths of life, the successes and failures, can cause us to feel distant from God. Our hope can appear to be all but gone as the obstacles in life mount high and the traumas of life run deep. The heights and the depths, the mountaintops and the valleys, may cause us to feel unsure of our hope, but the promise of Romans 8 is that there "ain't no mountain high enough, ain't no valley low enough . . . to keep me from you."

BOOM.

## Etcetera

The final adversary of hope stands alone, shrouded in the mist of fear and backlit by the bright and powerful love of Christ. All of the previous nine enemies of our hope have been defeated; all of the adversaries from the natural and the spiritual realms have been vanquished. Only one stands between us and undefeated hope: *"anything else in all creation."*

This seems to be, along with "powers" (the final term of verse 38), a theological etcetera. This phrase in particular seems to be a universal cover-all-the-bases final summary that Paul uses to eradicate any remaining doubt about the power and the presence of Christ's love. The comprehensive nature of this phrase has been interpreted to indicate that nothing in all creation, including other universes, undiscovered information, or even the creations of the creation can separate us from the love of God.

Undoubtedly we understand the emphasis here: There is nothing you can think of, discover, or one day realize that this list does not cover. We may at times be tempted to think that such things as evolutionary theory, a creation of modern man, might be able to destroy our hope. We may be tempted to think that the evils of our society—despicable and unthinkable behavior incomprehensible a century ago, unfathomable in Paul's day—may escape the scope of His love. We may even begin to believe that there is something in our lives that for the first time in the history of mankind could jeopardize His love for us.

KABOOM.

## The Epilogue of Hope

Even the most hopeful person needs to maintain that hope. A hope unrefreshed, unsustained, and unencouraged will eventually decay into hopelessness. As the Second Law of Thermodynamics teaches us, it will run down, run dry, and run out. That is the inevitable nature of living in a hope-denying, hope-defying, hope-draining world.

Christ has given us the commission and the tools to be the messengers of hope. We are not only responsible for maintaining our hope by our personal relationship with Him, but we are also responsible for contributing to the hope of others. It is Jesus Christ living in us who is the hope of glory, and we are the mechanics of hope. We are hope's contractors, hope's accountants and doctors, teachers and authors, counselors and representatives. We are the ones Jesus uses to build hope in others.

Time and nature conspire against hope. The longer hope remains neglected, the more in need of repair it becomes. We must participate in the reconstruction and maintenance of the hope of our families, friends, neighbors, churches, and communities. We are the agents of hope in a hopeless world. In fact, we are the exclusive distributors of genuine hope. The need is great, and the time is now.

Perhaps the most amazing feature of this responsibility is that in giving hope, our own hope is strengthened. The stronger we build someone else's hope, the stronger our own hope grows.

When you look to the future, where is your hope?

If not here, then where?

You may place your hope in a better society for a brighter future.

You may be willing to place your hope in social evolution or the inner power and deep-down goodness of your fellow man.

You may place your hope in institutions of government, higher education, medicine, counseling, social programs, criminal justice, and law enforcement.

You may look for your hope in wealth, technology, security, hard work, or intelligence.

You may look to your family, your friends, or your church to find hope.

You may even look in the mirror and find hope.

You may, and you are welcome to it.

No matter how advanced the science, no matter how progressive the ideas, no matter how powerful the institution, no matter how protective and pure the people, they cannot provide uncompromising, unfailing hope. While I may find encouragement and even confidence in institutions, powers, and people, they cannot provide me with a lasting hope.

Science will be outdated. Medicine will be confounded. Education will be forgotten. Wealth will be diminished. Kindness will be absent, and people will let you down. With all these things I will live, but in something else I will place my hope.

## ONE LAST HOPE

I only wish he could have heard those words one more time. I know he was familiar with them, and I know he had heard them before, perhaps many times. I don't know why they were not enough for him that day.

As we began our consideration of the subject of hope, I introduced you to a young man for whom a loss of hope turned out to be fatal. The tragedy of his suicide left his young children without a father and his young bride without a husband. His attempt to escape the darkness of his own hopelessness left his parents without their only son and his sisters without their only brother. His final and fatal choice that day, spoken in the language of violence, screamed out that he felt as if he himself were left alone in this world without any real hope.

Thanks be to God, we need never be.

# NOTES

## INTRODUCTION

1. Harry F. Waters, "Teenage Suicide: One Act Not to Follow," *Newsweek*, 18 April 1994, 49.

2. William Bennett, *The Index of Leading Cultural Indicators: Facts and Figures on the State of American Society* (New York: Simon & Schuster, 1994), 78-79.

3. Robert Wilonsky, "Small Apologies," *The Dallas Observer*, 14-20 April 1994, 58.

4. Bennett, *Index*, 22.

5. Bennett, *Index*, 23. Source: U.S. Department of Justice, Bureau of Justice Statistics, *Lifetime Likelihood of Victimization* (Washington, D.C.: U.S. Department of Justice, 1987).

6. Bennett, *Index*, 30. Source: U.S. Department of Justice, Office of the Attorney General, *Combating Violent Crime*, 1992.

7. Tom Morganthau, "It's Not Just New York . . . ," *Newsweek*, 2 March 1992, 26. Source: Ronald D. Stephens, National School Safety Center.

8. Lance Morrow, "Childhood's End," *Time*, 9 March 1992, 23.

9. Bennett, *Index*, 25. Source: Unpublished tabulations, U.S. National Center for Health Statistics, National Vital Statistics System, in Karl Zinsmeister, *Breakdown: How America's Fraying Family Ties Threaten Our Future*, 1995.

10. Barbara Kantrowitz, "Wild in the Streets," *Newsweek*, 2 August 1993, 43.

11. Ted Gest, "Crime Time Bomb," *U.S. News and World Report*, 25 March, 1996, 29.

12. Bennett, *Index*, 27. Source: U.S. Department of Justice, Bureau of Justice Statistics, *Sourcebook of Criminal Justice Statistics*, 1992 (Washington, D.C.: GPO, 1993).

13. Bennett, *Index*, 26. Source: Colin McCord and Harold Freeman, "Excess Mortality in Harlem," *The New England Journal of Medicine*, January 1990.

14. Gest, "Crime Time Bomb," 32.

15. George Barna, *Virtual America: What Every Christian Needs to Know About Ministering in an Age of Spiritual, Cultural and Technological Revolution* (Ventura, Calif: Regal Books, 1994), 83.

16. Barna, *Virtual America*, 93.

17. Barna, *Virtual America*, 83.

18. Barna, *Virtual America*, 83.

19. Job 13:15 (emphasis mine).

20. Psalm 33:16-20 (emphasis mine).

21. Isaiah 40:28-31 (emphasis mine).

22. Jeremiah 14:22 (emphasis mine).

23. 1 Peter 1:18-21 (emphasis mine).

24. Romans 8:22-25.

## 1 THE THIEF OF HOPE

1. Bob Costas, from an unpublished eulogy delivered at Mickey Mantle's funeral on Tuesday, August 15, 1995, at Lover's Lane United Methodist Church, Dallas Texas.

2. Baseball's Triple Crown goes to any player who finishes the season leading the league

in batting average, home runs, and runs batted in (RBIs). In 1956 Mantle won the Triple Crown with a .353 batting average, 52 home runs and 130 RBIs. Mantle's 52 home runs were the most hit by any Triple Crown winner. Since 1900 the Triple Crown has been accomplished fourteen times by twelve major league players. Only two men have won the Triple Crown since Mantle did it in 1956. The last Triple Crown winner was Carl Yastrzemski in 1967.

3.  Bob Costas, Eulogy.

4.  Roger Angell, "Superman in Pinstripes," *Time*, 21 August 1995, 72.

5.  Jack Kroll, "The Mantle of Greatness," *Newsweek*, 21 August 1995, 56.

6.  "The Fine Art of Chuckling" is included in most standard seminary curriculums. In this course, future pastors are instructed in the proper clerical responses of winking, nodding in agreement, and the all-important "Hmm." However, the pastoral handshake and appropriate forms of the famous "Bless you" are reserved for the more advanced classes, usually taken as electives. It is not recommended that laymen or seminary interns attempt a response to blatant sarcasm without years of practice or a senior pastoral staff member in a backup position.

7.  Mickey Mantle with Jill Lieber, "Time in a Bottle," *Sports Illustrated*, 18 April 1994, 74.

8.  David Falkner, *The Last Hero: The Life of Mickey Mantle* (New York: Simon & Schuster, 1995), 243-44.

## 2 THE HERO OF HOPE

1.  Jesus, in fact, reduced the ten commands to just two: "Love the LORD your God with all your heart and with all your soul and with all your strength" (Deut. 6:5), and "Love your neighbor as yourself" (Lev. 19:18). See Matthew 22:34-40.

2.  James D. G. Dunn, *Romans 1-8: The Word Biblical Commentary* (Dallas: Word Books, 1988), 38a:419-20.

3.  See 2 Corinthians 5:21; Galatians 4:4-5; Hebrews 4:15; 7:16; 9:28; 10:10.

4.  Hebrews 6:19-20, 4:14-16.

## 3 THE TEST OF HOPE

1.  I have no scientific evidence whatsoever to support this theory, nor do I have any credible psychological test data to confirm this opinion. The only basis upon which we can make a case for this psychobiological phenomenon is a strong sense of male intuition.

2.  George Barna, *If Things Are So Good, Why Do I Feel So Bad?* (Chicago: Moody Press, 1994), 196.

3.  Barna, *If Things Are So Good*, 197.

4.  Barna, *If Things Are So Good*, 8 (italics mine).

5.  Isaiah 64:6.

## 4 THE SPIRIT OF HOPE

1.  Daniel B. Wallace, "Who's Afraid of the Holy Spirit?" *Christianity Today*, 12 September 1994, 35.

2.  Gordon D. Fee, *God's Empowering Presence* (Peabody, Mass.: Hendrickson Publishers, 1994), 515.

3. The Greek word ζωοποιέω (*zopoieo*) is a literal combination of the words *life* and *to give*. Obviously, it means to give life. However, this is not life in its most generic sense, as in breathing and living, but life in its full, specifically spiritual sense, as in "spiritually alive."

4. Wallace, "Who's Afraid of the Holy Spirit?" 35-37.

## 5 THE ECONOMICS OF HOPE

1. Tom Heyman, *On an Average Day* (New York: Ballantine, 1989). These are average statistics from 1989. If we know anything about our society, it is that in most cases, the numbers are higher today than they were when this book was written.

2. Mark 9:43-47.

3. Genesis 39:6-7.

4. Genesis 39:8-10.

5. Genesis 39:11-12.

6. Emphasis mine.

7. 1 Corinthians 10:13.

## 6 THE PROMISE OF HOPE

1. John 8:31-59.

2. John 10:22-39.

3. The word συμμαρτυρέω (summartureo) is a combination of the word μαρτυρέω (martureo), meaning "to give testimony, to bear witness, to declare or to confirm" and the prefix συν (sun) meaning "in addition" or "with." The term μαρτυρέω (martureo) in its transliterated form is the English word *martyr*.

4. Genesis 12:2-3.

## 7 THE STRUGGLE OF HOPE

1. Philip Yancey, *Where Is God When It Hurts?* (Grand Rapids, Mich.: Zondervan, 1990).

2. The first word used here, ἀποκαραδοκία (*apokaradokia*), is used only one other time in the New Testament, in Philippians 1:20.

3. In the LXX translation of Genesis 3:16 the word οτεναγμός (*stenagmos*) is used, with the same implications as used here by Paul in Romans 8:22-23.

4. This type of chuckling (similar to the Pastoral Chuckle, see notes for chapter 1) is taught to all waiters at the finer restaurants and is encouraged in the pursuit of big tips, except in French restaurants and truck stops where scowling at the customers is not only encouraged but lifted to an art form.

5. The NIV translation does not use the word *hope* at all in the Pentateuch or Revelation. The word appears only once in the Gospels (in Matt. 12:21), and well over 70 percent of the Old Testament uses of the word occur in three books: Job (17 times), Psalms (31 times; 6 in Ps. 119) and Proverbs (11 times).

## 8 THE PRAYER OF HOPE

1. Scott O'Grady and Jeff Coplon, *Return with Honor* (New York: Doubleday Publishers, 1995), 28.

2. Ibid., 150-52.

3. Ibid., 173-74.

## 9 THE SUMMIT OF HOPE

1. The most common verbs in the New Testament for "to know" are οἶδα (*oida*), γινώσκω (*ginosko*), ἐπιγινώσκω (*epiginosko*), ἐπίσταμαι (*epistamai*) and γνωρίζω (*gnorizo*), along with a number of other terms translated "to know" or "to understand." There is a subtlety in meaning to each term related primarily to two factors: 1) the source of the knowledge, 2) the relationship between the one who knows and the thing known. Of all of these terms οἶδα (*oida*) most often implies an intuitive sense of understanding that is affirmed rather than learned by experience.

2. What I found out later is that this small yellow paperlike plane called a *Citaborea* is specifically designed for acrobatics. In fact, the name *Citaborea* is *aerobatic* spelled backwards. I will make sure that I never fly in an airplane without getting its correct spelling first. This may be the reason that a company like Boeing calls its aircraft things like 707, 727, 737, 747, and so forth, which both backwards and forwards sound safe. Who knows—someone may one day make a plane called a *Hsarc*.

3. The Greek term is συνεργέω (*sunergeo*), which is the combination of the prefix σύν (*sun*) meaning "with" and ενεργέω (*energeo*), meaning "energy or work." It literally means "to work together."

4. Clarence L. Barnhart, ed. in chief, *The World Book Dictionary*, vol. 2 (Chicago: Thorndike Barnhardt, 1967), 1,985.

5. The word προγινώσκω (*proginosko*) is a combination of the prefix πρό (*pro*), "before," and γινώσκω (*ginosko*), "to know."

6. William Sanday and Arthur Headlam, *A Critical and Exegetical Commentary on the Epistle to the Romans,* The International Critical Commentary (Edinburgh: T. & T. Clark, 1980), 217.

7. John MacArthur, *Romans 1-8,* The MacArthur New Testament Commentary (Chicago: Moody Press, 1991), 496.

8. Matthew 8:18; Mark 4:35; Luke 8:22.

9. Matthew 8:24; Mark 4:37.

10. Matthew 8:24; Mark 4:38; Luke 8:23.

11. Mark 4:38.

12. John Hunt, *The Ascent of Everest* (Seattle: The Mountaineers, 1993), 186-87.

13. Ibid., 212.

## 10 THE ROLLER COASTER OF HOPE

1. Todd H. Throgmorton, *Roller Coasters of America* (Osceloa, Wisc.: Motorbooks International Publishers, 1994), 113-22.

## 11 THE STANDING OVATION OF HOPE

1. Philippians 2:10-11.

2. Acts 14:1-18.

3. 2 Corinthians 12:2-4.

# SELECTED BIBLIOGRAPHY

## A. PRIMARY COMMENTARIES ON ROMANS

Barclay, William. *The Letter to the Romans*. The Daily Bible Study Series. Rev. ed. Philadelphia: The Westminster Press, 1975.

Barton, Bruce B., David R. Veerman, and Neil Wilson. *Romans*. The Life Application Bible Commentary. Ed. Grant Osborne. Wheaton, Ill.: Tyndale House Publishers, Inc., 1992.

Boice, James Montgomery. *Romans: Volume 2, "The Reign of Grace" Romans 5:1-8:39*. Grand Rapids: Baker Book House, 1992.

Briscoe, D. Stuart. *Romans*. The Communicator's Commentary. Waco, Tex.: Word Publishing Company, 1982.

Bruce, F. F. *The Epistle of Paul to the Romans*. The Tyndale New Testament Commentaries. Grand Rapids: Wm. B. Eerdmans Publishing Company, 1963.

Cranfield, C. E. B. *A Critical and Exegetical Commentary on the Epistle to the Romans*. The International Critical Commentary. Vol. 1. Edinburgh: T. & T. Clark, 1982.

Dunn, James D. G. *Romans 1-8: The Word Biblical Commentary*. Vol. 38A. Waco, Tex.: Word Publishing Company, 1988.

Harrison, Everett F. *Romans*. The Expositor's Bible Commentary. Vol. 10. Ed. Frank E. Gaebelein. Grand Rapids: Zondervan Publishing House, 1976.

Hendriksen, William. *Exposition of Paul's Epistle to the Romans*, New Testament Commentary Series. Grand Rapids: Baker Book House, 1980.

MacArthur, John F. *Romans 1-8*. The MacArthur New Testament Commentary. Chicago: Moody Press, 1991.

Moo, Douglas. *Romans 1-8*. The Wycliffe Exegetical Commentary. Chicago: Moody Press, 1991.

Sanday, William and Arthur C. Headlam. *A Critical and Exegetical Commentary on the Epistle to the Romans*. The International Critical Commentary. Edinburgh: T. & T. Clark, 1992.

Shedd, William G. T. *Commentary on Romans*. Grand Rapids: Baker Book House, 1980.

Sproul, R. C. *Romans: Focus on the Bible*. Geanies House, Scotland: Christian Focus Publications Ltd., 1994.

Wiersbe, Warren W. *Be Right*. Wheaton, Ill.: Victor Books, 1977.

## B. RELATED THEOLOGICAL RESOURCES

Fee, Gordon D. *God's Empowering Presence: The Holy Spirit in the Letters of Paul*. Peabody, Mass.: Hendrickson Publishers, 1994.

Lindsey, Hal. *The Terminal Generation*. Old Tappan, N.J.: Flemming H. Revell Company, 1976.

## C. SELECTED TOPICAL WORKS — "HOPE"

Crabb, Lawrence J. and Dan B. Allender. *Encouragement: The Key to Caring*. Grand Rapids: Zondervan Publishing House, 1984.

Dobson, James. *When God Doesn't Make Sense*. Wheaton, Ill.: Tyndale House Publishers, Inc., 1993.

Jeremiah, David. *Acts of Love: The Power of Encouragement*. Gresham, Ore.: Vision House Publishing, Inc., 1994.

Lewis, Clive Staples. *A Grief Observed*. San Francisco: HarperCollins Publishers, 1961.

McCullough, Donald W. *The Trivialization of God: The Dangerous Illusion of a Manageable Deity*. Colorado Springs: NavPress, 1995.

MacArthur, John F. *The Power of Suffering*. Wheaton, Ill.: Victor Books, 1995.

———. *Anxiety Attacked*. Wheaton, Ill.: Victor Books, 1993.

Minirith, Frank, Paul Meier, and Don Hawkins. *Worry-Free Living*. Nashville: Thomas Nelson Publishers, 1989.

Yancey, Philip. *Disappointment with God: Three Questions No One Asks Aloud*. Grand Rapids: Zondervan Publishing House, 1992.

———. *Finding God in Unexpected Places*. Nashville: Moorings, 1995.

———. *Where Is God When It Hurts?* Grand Rapids: Zondervan Publishing House, 1990.

## D. SELECTED WORKS—CULTURAL ANALYSIS

Barna, George. *Baby Busters: The Disillusioned Generation*. Chicago: Northfield Publishing, 1992.

———. *If Things Are So Good, Why Do I Feel So Bad?* Chicago: Moody Press, 1994.

———. *The Frog in the Kettle: What Christians Need to Know About Life in the Year 2000*. Ventura: Regal Books, 1990.

———. *Virtual America: What Every Christian Needs to Know About Ministering in an Age of Spiritual, Cultural and Technological Revolution*. Ventura: Regal Books, 1994.

———. *What Americans Believe*. Ventura: Regal Books, 1991.

Bennett, William J. *The De-Valuing of America: The Fight for Our Culture and Our Children*. Colorado Springs: Focus on the Family Publishers, 1994.

———. *The Index of Leading Cultural Indicators: Facts and Figures on the State of American Society*. New York: Simon & Schuster, 1994.

Naisbitt, John and Patricia Aburdene. *Megatrends 2000: Ten New Directions for the 1990s*. New York: William Morrow and Company Inc., 1990.

## E. SELECTED WORKS—ILLUSTRATIVE RESOURCES

Falkner, David. *The Last Hero: The Life of Mickey Mantle*. New York: Simon & Schuster Inc., 1995.

Hawking, Stephen. *A Brief History of Time: From the Big Bang to Black Holes*. New York: Bantam Books, 1990.

Herskowitz, Mickey. *Mickey Mantle: An Appreciation*. New York: William Morrow and Company, Inc., 1995.

Heyman, Tom. *On an Average Day*. New York: Ballantine Books, 1989.

Hunt, John. *The Ascent of Everest*. Seattle: The Mountaineers, 1993.

Lovell, Jim, and Jeffrey Kluger. *Apollo 13* (Previously titled *Lost Moon*). New York: Pocket Books, 1995.

O'Grady, Scott, and Jeff Coplon. *Return with Honor*. New York: Doubleday Publishers, 1995.

Rookmaaker, H. R. *Modern Art and the Death of a Culture*. Wheaton, Ill.: Crossway Books, 1994.

Sagan, Carl. *The Demon-Haunted World: Science as a Candle in the Dark*. New York: Random House Publishers, 1995.

Throgmorton, Todd H. *Roller Coasters of America*. Osceola, Wisc.: Motorbooks International Publishers, 1994.